MODERN
FRENCH PASTRY

PAGE STREET
PUBLISHING CO.

Copyright © 2017 Cheryl Wakerhauser

First published in 2017 by
Page Street Publishing Co.
27 Congress Street, Suite 105
Salem, MA 01970
www.pagestreetpublishing.com

Distributed by Macmillan, sales in Canada by The Canadian Manda Group.

22   21   20   19   18   3 4 5 6 7

ISBN-13: 978-1-62414-437-0
ISBN-10: 1-62414-437-3

Library of Congress Control Number: 2017938390

Cover and book design by Page Street Publishing Co.
Photography by Alan Weiner

Printed and bound in China

MODERN FRENCH PASTRY

Innovative Techniques, Tools and Design

CHERYL WAKERHAUSER, owner of Pix Pâtisserie

PAGE STREET
PUBLISHING CO.

CONTENTS

INTRODUCTION

WHAT IS FRENCH PASTRY?

Opéra, Tarte au Citron, Mont Blanc . . . quintessential classic French pastries. I remember my first visit to Paris (there have been many since), when I took a photo with every dessert I ate. They were just so beautiful—exquisitely decorated, colorful and presented in jewelry box–like pastry cases. But certainly not too pretty to eat, with every bite bursting with a myriad of textures and seductive flavors. These were not brownies. This was not pie. And certainly, they were no cupcakes.

Most popular American desserts are two dimensional—cake and frosting, pie and crust, dare I say . . . Jell-O and whipped cream. You have two flavors and two textures. They are often overly sweet, which may be why some people insist they don't like dessert. Presentation can be less than stellar—a cut-up cake fallen over on a plate has no resemblance to its whole counterpart.

The deep-rooted pastry culture in France is much different. To them, it's an art. To them, it's tradition. To them, there is more to dessert than sugar. The pastry profession is an honored craft. Driven pâtissiers spend years of their lives training for a three-day test to become a Meilleur Ouvrier de France—the best worker of their craft. Even those that don't accomplish the daunting feat take their daily work very seriously. I've worked alongside rugby players pulling beautiful sugar roses at four in the morning and teenagers working long hours as stagiaires (interns) unmolding bûche de noël after bûche de noël in preparation for Christmas. It is a labor of love and it shows.

When you walk into a pâtisserie in France, the desserts in the pastry cases will captivate you. Rows upon rows of slender éclairs, colorful macarons and tarts piled high with wild strawberries, physalis and red currants. Each dessert is like a little package or gift, crafted individually so you don't have to share, and decorated as if it were going in a museum, not in your mouth. When you do take a bite you can expect something crunchy, something creamy, perhaps a crack of caramel or a soft, tender cake soaked in rum. The flavors can be bold, or slightly flirtatious, but there will always be many. Aside from their beauty, it is the layering of many textures and flavors you get in every bite that sets French pâtisserie apart from other desserts. It is this multidimensionality that make them complex and so enjoyable, a bit like a fine wine.

SECRETS TO SUCCESS

Let's be honest, creating French-style desserts can be difficult and a bit intimidating. Macarons have only three ingredients, but time and time again, attempts to make them are unsuccessful. The success of pastry making relies on technique, quality ingredients and having the right equipment.

This book will guide you through the basic techniques commonly used in French pastry. Learn the difference between French meringue and Italian meringue. Prepare a proper caramel. Temper chocolate in your microwave. Although some of the recipes may seem a bit daunting in length, the results are well worth it and you will be amazed at what you've accomplished. Once you have mastered the techniques, take components from one dessert and combine them with components from another to create your own masterpiece. The possibilities are unlimited.

Not all chocolates are created equal and sugar can come from beets or cane. The importance of choosing fresh, high-quality ingredients will be reflected in your results. If you start with subpar, it's not going to get any better.

Equally important is the equipment you choose. Since pastry is part art, part science, precision is of the utmost importance. That is why all ingredients in this book are measured on a scale. I cannot stress enough the importance of weighing your ingredients versus using cups and spoons. If ten people scoop a cup of all-purpose flour and put it on a scale they will all weigh differently. Yet if that same ten weighed 100 grams of all-purpose flour on a scale, everyone would have exactly the same amount of flour. If the recipe calls for 100 grams of flour, that's what it needs, not 115 grams. If you have a recipe that calls for three large eggs and you have only medium eggs, what do you do? If instead, the recipe calls for 150 grams of eggs, you simply add enough beaten medium eggs until the scale reads 150 grams. Easy and simple. A digital scale will be your new best friend.

ODDS AND ENDS

Every recipe in this book lists ingredients by weight in grams, including liquid ingredients. If you are unfamiliar with metric, don't worry. All you need to do is put your ingredients on the scale. That's it!

Here are some general measurements to get you accustomed to thinking in metric:

1 large egg = 50 g (20 g for the yolk and 30 g for the white). If you need to measure partial eggs, say 130 g, crack three eggs in a bowl, break them up with a fork and pour 130 g into your recipe.

1 cup of flour = 130 g

1 cup of sugar = 200 g

1 cup of heavy cream = 255 g

1 packet of powdered gelatin = 7 g

NOTE: You can substitute sheet gelatin by weight one to one. Ignore the water listed in the recipe and use enough cold water to submerge the sheets. Excess water not absorbed will be rung out.

All baking instructions are for still, conventional ovens that do not have a fan. If you have a convection oven and want to bake with the fan on, just lower the temperature by 25°F (14°C). Baking times may be a bit faster, so check the product earlier than noted.

Some recipes require mixing very small quantities. Depending on the size of your stand mixer's bowl, the attachment may barely reach the ingredients. Prop the bowl up slightly by placing a towel over one or both of the pegs that hold the bowl, before attaching it to the mixer, making sure it is secured in the back. That's what we call a Parlor Trick!

Throughout the book you will see PARLOR TRICK! This is where we offer tips and shortcuts, sometimes debunking classic techniques, such as making pastry cream in the microwave. Why dirty several dishes, stand there stirring for five minutes and risk burning your pastry cream? Instead, place everything in one bowl, place it in the microwave and walk away. No risk of burning and no muscles required.

Finally, it is strongly recommended that you read the entire recipe and weigh all your ingredients before starting any dessert. A successful pâtissier is always a well-organized one.

For more detailed information about equipment and ingredients used in this book, visit www.modernfrenchpastry.com.

CHAPTER ONE

CAKES

This chapter focuses on different styles and flavors of cakes—vanilla or chocolate, fluffy or dense, almond or flourless. The cakes then become the base of dessert creations that are so much more than traditional birthday cake. None of the cakes contain any baking soda or baking powder, which are rarely used in French pastry. Instead, the French will used whipped egg whites, whipped egg yolks or both to give lightness to a cake. It is also customary to soak your cake with a flavored syrup to keep it moist.

PISTACHIO PICNIC CAKE

DIFFICULTY:

Perfect for a picnic or summer barbecue.

This dessert is relatively easy to make and the pistachio and almond pastes really pack it with a burst of flavor. The pistachio cake is a moist, barely sweet, dense nut cake. Crème légère translates to "light cream." Here we are making a basic pastry cream and then lightening it with whipped cream. The combination of the dense cake, light cream and fresh berries is the perfect trifecta.

You can make your own pistachio paste by grinding pistachios in a food processor, but start with 50 grams of pistachios to account for any loss in the process. It takes a while to get to paste consistency.

For this recipe you will need a 20 centimeter (8 in) cake ring.

YIELD: 10 servings

PISTACHIO ALMOND CAKE

300 g almond paste

30 g pistachio paste

210 g eggs

25 g all-purpose flour

25 g cornstarch

90 g unsalted butter, melted

Preheat the oven to 375°F (190°C). Place a 20-centimeter (8-in) metal cake ring on a half sheet pan lined with a silicone baking mat.

Place the almond and pistachio pastes in the bowl of a stand mixer fitted with the paddle attachment. Mix on medium speed until combined. Slowly add the eggs in 3 parts, scraping the bowl after each addition. When all the eggs are incorporated, increase the mixer speed to high and whisk until light and fluffy, about 4 minutes.

Sift together the flour and cornstarch. Decrease the mixer speed to low and add the dry ingredients. Once incorporated, add the butter and mix until just combined.

Pour the batter into the cake ring and place a second half sheet pan underneath the first. Bake until lightly browned and the top of the cake is firm to the touch, about 20 minutes. The cake will pull away from the cake ring and fall slightly as it cools.

KIRSCH SOAKING SYRUP

200 g Soaking Syrup (page 198)

40 g kirsch (cherry brandy)

Combine the syrup with the kirsch. Set aside.

VANILLA BEAN CRÈME LÉGÈRE

½ vanilla bean

500 g milk

100 g egg yolks

125 g sugar

50 g cornstarch

25 g unsalted butter

180 g heavy cream

Prepare a pastry cream by cutting the vanilla bean in half again lengthwise. Scrape out the seeds and place them in a small saucepan with the milk. Bring to a boil and then remove from the heat.

Put the egg yolks in a medium bowl. Add the sugar and cornstarch to the egg yolks and immediately whisk until the mixture turns pale, about 10 seconds. Slowly whisk the milk into the egg mixture and then strain it into a clean saucepan.

Over medium heat, whisk continually until the mixture starts to thicken. Pull off the heat and keep whisking while the mixture continues to thicken from the residual heat. Return the pan to the heat, still whisking, until the mixture boils, being careful not to burn the bottom. Remove from the heat, add the butter and stir until it melts. Pour the pastry cream into a shallow bowl and place plastic wrap directly on top of the cream to prevent a skin from forming. Refrigerate immediately.

Once cold, transfer the pastry cream to the bowl of the stand mixer fitted with the paddle attachment. Mix on high speed until smooth, about 30 seconds.

In a separate mixer bowl, using the whisk attachment, whisk the heavy cream to stiff peak. Fold it into the softened pastry cream.

ASSEMBLY

50 g pistachios

200 g fresh raspberries

Run the back of a small offset spatula around the inside of the cake ring to loosen it and remove the cake. Turn the cake upside down onto a half sheet pan lined with parchment.

Heat the kirsch syrup until hot. Generously brush the cake with the syrup. Place a cake board or platter on top, lift up the sheet pan and flip the cake over. Remove the sheet pan and soak the other side of the cake generously with the syrup.

Chop 40 grams of the pistachios. Using an offset spatula, spread a thin layer of vanilla crème légère over the top and around the sides of the cake. While holding the cake off the table with one hand, press the chopped pistachios to the side of the cake until they stick. Layer 175 grams of the raspberries on the top of the cake, leaving the outer 2 centimeters (0.75 in) uncovered. Spread 250 grams of the crème légère into a mound over the raspberries. Using a piping bag fitted with a 1.25-centimeter (0.5-in) open tip, pipe small dollops of cream around the outer edge, then cover the whole center. Sprinkle the top with more chopped pistachios and decorate with whole pistachios and raspberries.

CHERRY BOMB

DIFFICULTY: 🍪 🍪

Leftover cherries? Make a Manhattan.

Amarena cherries are gown in the Emilia-Romagna region of Italy. They are dark in color with a slight bitter note, but when preserved in sugar syrup, as they are usually found, they have a lovely intense sweet cherry flavor. The overprocessed, neon red maraschino cherries on grocery store shelves are no comparison, and no substitute!

The cake featured in this recipe has an intense chocolate flavor but still manages to be light on the palate. The use of invert sugar helps keep this cake extremely delicate and moist. If you cannot find invert sugar, substitute honey.

Avoid the temptation to bake the cake in the 20-centimeter (8-in) cake ring used in the assembly, or else you will end up over cooking it and it will be very dense.

For this recipe, you will need a 20-centimeter (8-in) cake ring, 5 centimeters (2 in) tall, with acetate for molding and various sizes of demisphere polycarbonate molds to make the gold sphere décor.

YIELD: 10 servings

CHOCOLATE ALMOND CAKE

100 g dark chocolate

90 g unsalted butter

65 g all-purpose flour

30 g powdered sugar

30 g almond meal

75 g egg yolks

55 g invert sugar, warm

150 g egg whites

35 g brown sugar

Preheat the oven to 375°F (190°C). Line a half sheet pan with a silicone baking mat.

In a microwave-safe bowl, melt the chocolate and butter in the microwave on low, stirring often.

Sift the flour and powdered sugar into the bowl of a stand mixer fitted with the whisk attachment. Add the almond meal, egg yolks and invert sugar and whisk on high speed until pale, about 3 minutes. Place this mixture in a larger bowl and set aside.

Prepare a French meringue (see page 191) with the egg whites and brown sugar, whisking to stiff peak. Take a fourth of the meringue and stir it into the egg yolk mixture. This will loosen up the mixture and allow the rest of the meringue to incorporate easier. Fold in half of the remaining meringue and then the final half. Fold in the melted chocolate mixture.

Spread evenly onto the half sheet pan, using an offset spatula. Bake until dry to the touch and just barely firm, about 10 to 12 minutes. Do not overbake. This cake will be very soft and fragile, so after it cools, place it in the freezer for easier handling.

CINNAMON STREUSEL

80 g unsalted butter

65 g brown sugar

65 g almond meal

80 g pastry flour

Pinch of salt

1 g (½ tsp) ground cinnamon

70 g dark chocolate

Preheat the oven to 350°F (175°C). Line a half sheet pan with a silicone baking mat.

Mix the butter with the brown sugar in the bowl of the stand mixer fitted with the paddle attachment on medium speed until well combined, about 2 minutes.

Stir together the almond meal, pastry flour, salt and cinnamon in a bowl and then add them to the butter mixture. Mix on low speed until the dough starts clumping together, about 1 minute. Remove the dough from the bowl and form it into a single mass.

Break off randomly shaped pieces about the size of a hazelnut and place them on the pan in a single layer. Bake until lightly golden brown, 12 to 14 minutes.

Once the streusel is cool, melt the chocolate. Add just 80 grams of the streusel to the chocolate and stir until the streusel is completely coated. Spread in a single layer on a half sheet pan lined with parchment. Place the chocolate streusel in the refrigerator and chill until the chocolate is set, about 5 minutes. Remove it from the refrigerator and set aside at room temperature.

MILK CHOCOLATE GLAZE

8 g powdered gelatin

40 g cold water

75 g water

150 g glucose syrup or corn syrup

100 g sweetened condensed milk

150 g milk chocolate

Red food coloring, as desired

In a small bowl, combine the gelatin with the cold water and stir well to dissolve. Let sit for 5 minutes to bloom.

In a small saucepan over medium-high heat, cook the remaining 75 grams of water and the glucose to 217°F (103°C). Remove from the heat and pour into a small bowl along with the condensed milk. Add the gelatin and the chocolate and let sit for 1 minute, then mix with an immersion blender until smooth. Add red food coloring, little by little, mixing until a desired shade is reached. Reserve at room temperature.

CHOCOLATE CREAM

80 g egg yolks

200 g heavy cream

200 g milk

28 g dark alkalized cocoa powder

40 g sugar

190 g dark chocolate

Place the egg yolks in a medium bowl. Combine the cream, milk, cocoa powder and sugar in a small saucepan and heat to 185°F (85°C). Slowly pour the milk mixture over the yolks while whisking. Add the chocolate and wait for 1 minute for it to soften, then blend with an immersion blender until smooth.

GOLD CHOCOLATE SPHERES

800 g dark chocolate

Gold leaf, as needed

Temper the chocolate in the microwave (see Techniques, page 190). Pour the chocolate into the demisphere mold to fill all the cavities. Tap the mold on the edge of the counter fast and vigorously for a few seconds, to release any air bubbles. Flip the mold upside down, holding it over a piece of parchment. Tap the side of the mold with a wide metal scraper to get rid of the excess chocolate. Scrape the top of the mold smooth and place it upside down on a clean piece of parchment.

After 1 minute, lift up the mold and scrape the top clean with the metal scraper. Place it right side up in the refrigerator and chill for 5 minutes, to set the chocolate. Repeat with the second mold. Remove the molds from the refrigerator and let sit for another 10 minutes.

Slide half of the demispheres out of the mold. Heat the metal scraper with a propane torch. Holding the demisphere flat on the surface of the scraper, melt the edges. Piece the melted edges together with the edges of one of the demispheres still in the mold. Continue until all the spheres are complete. Let sit 5 minutes at room temperature. Wrap in the gold leaf.

PARLOR TRICK! To get the gold leaf to stick to the chocolate spheres, try this tip! Spike the chocolate spheres with toothpicks. Fill a wide bowl, 10 centimeters (4 in) deep, with cool water and place it on a stool just below the counter edge. Open a book of gold leaf to reveal a full sheet and place it on the counter just above the water. Pinch the front corners of the sheet of gold leaf and slowly drag it onto the surface of the water. Plunge the chocolate into the center of the gold leaf and down under the surface of the water. While it is still underwater, turn the chocolate right side up and push it up out of the water. Place the toothpick into a piece of Styrofoam and allow the sphere to dry completely, about 1 hour.

Carefully drag a sheet of gold leaf over the surface of the water.

The gold leaf will stick to the surface. Magical, right?

Plunge the chocolate sphere into the center of the sheet of gold leaf and submerge it under water.

Turn the sphere right side up before pushing it back up out of the water.

ASSEMBLY

Cocoa powder, as needed

150 g Amarena cherries

Sugar, for dusting

Strain off and discard any liquid.

Remove the chocolate cake from the freezer. Lightly dust the cake top with granulated sugar so it will not stick when unmolding. Cut around the edges to break the cake away from the sides of the pan. Place a piece of parchment over the cake and flip it upside down. Peel back the silicone mat slowly, starting at one corner and pulling the mat not up, but almost parallel to the mat itself in the opposite direction.

Using a 20-centimeter (8-in) cake ring, cut 2 circles from the cake and set aside. Place the cake ring on a parchment-lined half sheet pan and line the ring with acetate. Use the remainder of the cake to piece together a flat bottom layer in the cake ring (you get to eat anything that doesn't fit!). Top with half of the chocolate cream (about 340 grams). Sink the cherries, one by one, into the cream, creating a layer of cherry-studded chocolate cream.

Place one of the cake disks on top of the cherry-studded chocolate cream and press firmly. Top with the remaining chocolate cream and now sink the chocolate-covered streusel into it to create a layer of streusel-studded chocolate cream. Top with the final cake disk, press firmly and freeze overnight.

Once frozen, remove the cake ring and acetate. Place the cake on a wire rack over a clean sheet pan. Warm the milk chocolate glaze to 95°F (35°C). Pour the glaze quickly and generously over the top and sides. Using a large offset spatula, push the glaze once to level it off, letting the excess fall over the edges. Lift up the cake, using a large offset spatula, and place it on a cake board or platter. Dust the non-chocolate coated streusel pieces with cocoa powder and stick them around the base of the cake, going up the sides about 2.5 centimeters (1 in). Top the cake with the gold chocolate spheres and a few more pieces of streusel.

CANCALE

DIFFICULTY:

Seaside. Brittany. That's where you want to be.

A bit of Americana layered with French technique. The joconde biscuit is the cake used to make the classic French Opéra dessert. It is also used as a side décor in many entremets. Take care when folding the ingredients together, as you want to maintain as much volume in the batter as possible.

For the cheesecake mousse, it is highly recommended to seek out a top-quality cream cheese, such as Sierra Nevada's Gina Marie from California, or one from your local cheese shop or farmers' market. The ubiquitous grocery store brand just doesn't offer the same flavor.

YIELD: 12 servings

JOCONDE BISCUIT

Pan release spray

130 g powdered sugar

70 g pastry flour

130 g blanched almond meal

180 g eggs

240 g egg whites

60 g granulated sugar

30 g unsalted butter, melted

Preheat the oven to 425°F (218°C). Line 2 very flat half sheet pans with silicone baking mats. Spray with pan release.

Sift the powdered sugar and flour into the bowl of a stand mixer fitted with the paddle attachment. Add the almond meal and stir to combine. Add the eggs and beat on high speed until the batter is light and fluffy, about 4 minutes. Place this mixture in a larger bowl and set aside.

In the clean bowl of the stand mixer now fitted with the whisk attachment, make a French meringue (see page 191) by whisking the egg whites and granulated sugar until just firm. Do not overwhisk, or else the meringue will become crumbly and not incorporate into the batter well. Very gently, fold half of the meringue into the almond mixture, followed by the butter and then the remaining meringue.

Divide the batter between the 2 half sheet pans (about 370 grams per sheet). Spread the batter with a large offset spatula, making sure you have an even thickness across the pan. Bake for about 12 minutes, rotating once after 6 minutes. The cake is done when the top springs back and is dry to the touch and just starting to brown. If overcooked, the cake will become crunchy toward the edges or in shallow spots.

Place half of the meringue in the bowl with the batter.

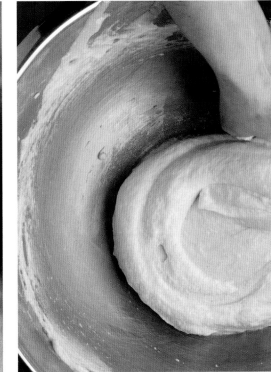

Gently fold.

Add the melted butter.

Fold in the remaining meringue.

BLUEBERRY COULIS

14 g powdered gelatin

70 g cold water

600 g blueberry puree

130 g sugar

Pan release spray

Line a very flat half sheet pan lined with a silicone mat.

In a small bowl, combine the gelatin with the cold water and stir well to dissolve. Let sit for 5 minutes to bloom.

Combine the puree and sugar in a small saucepan and heat just until warm and the sugar is dissolved, about 3 minutes. Add the solid gelatin mass to the puree and stir until the gelatin is melted, then pour the mixture onto the half sheet pan. Spread the coulis as evenly as possible (tapping the pan bottom on the counter also helps) and place it in the freezer. Freeze for at least 4 hours.

Cut along the edges to release the coulis from the pan. Spray a piece of parchment with pan release and place it, sprayed side down, on the coulis. Flip the pan over and remove the pan. Remove the silicone mat, cut the coulis and the parchment in half widthwise and place back in the freezer. Freeze until assembly.

CHEESECAKE MOUSSE

14 g cornstarch

520 g cream cheese

160 g sugar

5 g lime zest (from 2 limes)

210 g sour cream

185 g eggs

3 g (¾ tsp) vanilla extract

7 g powdered gelatin

35 g cold water

200 g heavy cream

Preheat the oven to 300°F (150°C). Place a silicone baking mat on a half sheet pan.

Sift the cornstarch into the bowl of the stand mixer fitted with the paddle attachment. Add the cream cheese, sugar and zest to the bowl and mix on medium speed until smooth, about 2 minutes. In a separate small bowl, whisk together the sour cream with the eggs and vanilla. Add a third of this mixture to the cream cheese. Scrape down the side of the bowl and mix on high speed until combined. Add the next third, scrape down the sides of the bowl and then mix to combine, then repeat again with the remaining third.

Pour the batter onto the half sheet pan. Bake until set, about 18 minutes. The cake may still be wet to the touch, but when the pan is tilted, the cake should not move. While the cheesecake is baking, whisk the cream to soft peaks.

Scrape the warm cheesecake into the bowl of the stand mixer fitted with the paddle attachment. Mix on high speed until smooth, about 15 seconds.

In a small bowl, combine the gelatin with the cold water and stir well to dissolve. Let sit for 5 minutes to bloom.

Melt the gelatin in a small microwave-safe bowl on low in the microwave. Swirl the bowl every 30 seconds to stir the gelatin, until it is completely melted. While mixing on low speed, add the melted gelatin to the warm cheesecake mousse. Scrape down the sides of the bowl and make sure it is well combined. Fold in the whipped cream. Use immediately (see Assembly, page 25).

LIME SYRUP

300 g Soaking Syrup (page 198)

50 g fresh lime juice (from about 2 limes)

In a medium bowl, combine the syrup with the lime juice. Set aside.

WHITE CHOCOLATE GLAZE

8 g powdered gelatin

40 g cold water

75 g water

150 g sugar

150 g glucose syrup or corn syrup

100 g sweetened condensed milk

150 g white chocolate

Blue food coloring, as desired

In a small bowl, combine the gelatin with the cold water and stir well to dissolve. Let sit for 5 minutes to bloom.

In a small saucepan over medium-high heat, cook the remaining 75 grams of water and the sugar and glucose to 217°F (103°C). Remove from the heat and pour into a small bowl along with the condensed milk. Add the gelatin and the chocolate and let sit for 1 minute, then mix with an immersion blender until smooth. Add the blue food coloring, little by little, mixing until a desired shade is reached. Reserve at room temperature.

ASSEMBLY

Sugar, for dusting

Blueberries, as needed

Silver leaf, as needed

Lightly dust the joconde cake top with granulated sugar so it will not stick when unmolding. Cut around the edges to break the cake away from the sides of the pan. Place a piece of parchment over each cake and flip the cakes upside down. Peel off the silicone mats slowly, starting at one corner and pulling the mat not up, but almost parallel to the mat itself in the opposite direction. If the cake is sticking or breaking, place it in the freezer to chill for 15 minutes and try again. Cut each cake in half widthwise, leaving 4 rectangles of approximately 20 x 28 centimeters (8 x 11 in).

Place one cake layer on a clean piece of parchment, bottom of the cake facing up. Heat the lime syrup until hot and brush the cake generously with it. Top with one-third (about 360 grams) of the cheesecake mousse and spread all the way to the edges as evenly as possible. Carefully place one of the frozen coulis pieces on top of the mousse, using the parchment to pick it up and flip it over.

Top with a second piece of cake and brush generously with lime syrup. Spread the next third of the cheesecake mousse evenly on top.

Top with a third piece of cake and brush generously with lime syrup. Top with the second piece of coulis and gently press to flatten. Spread the final third of the cheesecake mousse evenly on top. Cover with the last piece of cake and soak generously with syrup. Freeze the cake.

In a small saucepan, warm the glaze to 93°F (34°C). Place the frozen cake on a cutting board. Pour the glaze quickly and generously over the top to cover completely, letting the excess run off the edges. Place the cake back in the freezer for 10 minutes to allow the glaze to firm up. Remove from the freezer and trim all 4 sides with a long knife, to reveal the layers. Be sure to wipe your knife clean after each cut. For individual servings, cut the cake into thirds widthwise. Then, cut each of the 3 rows into 4 pieces approximately 9 x 5 centimeters (3.5 x 2 in). Decorate with blueberries and silver leaf.

BASTILLE

DIFFICULTY:

The only way to eat this cake is to storm it with your fork.

The quintessential cake in French pastry is the génoise. It is an extremely versatile, light sponge cake that is usually soaked with a syrup to add flavor and keep it moist. Care must be taken when mixing and spreading the batter. Once your eggs obtain their beautiful volume, try to incorporate the flour and butter with as little folding as possible, so the cake remains light and airy.

YIELD: 10 servings

GÉNOISE

340 g eggs

190 g sugar, plus more for dusting

190 g pastry flour

60 g unsalted butter, melted

Preheat the oven to 350°F (175°C). Line a half sheet pan with a silicone baking mat.

Place 2.5 centimeters (1 in) of water in a small saucepan and bring it to a simmer. In the bowl of a stand mixer, whisk the eggs and sugar by hand to combine. Place the bowl over the pot of simmering water and heat, whisking constantly, until the mixture reaches 105°F (40°C).

Immediately remove the bowl from the heat and transfer it to the mixer. Whisk on high speed, using the whisk attachment, until the bottom of the bowl is cool to the touch and the batter is light and fluffy, about 5 minutes. When the whisk is removed, the batter should fall on itself without sinking.

Transfer the batter into a very large bowl with a wide surface area on top. Sift one-fourth of the flour onto the batter in a thin layer covering the top. Gently fold the flour into the batter and then repeat, one-fourth at a time, until all the flour is incorporated. Pour the melted butter over the top and fold just until combined. Do not overmix. Ideally, if you have a helper in the kitchen, have the person continually sift the flour over the batter while you continually fold. If you add too much flour at once, it could clump up in the batter.

Pour the batter onto the half sheet pan and spread evenly, using a large offset spatula. Bake until the top is dry to the touch and golden brown, about 18 to 20 minutes.

ORANGE CREAM

75 g unsalted butter

170 g orange juice

8 g orange zest, finely zested

120 g egg yolks

100 g eggs

100 g sugar

Pinch of salt

Place a strainer over a medium bowl and set aside. Melt the butter over low heat in a small saucepan. Add the remaining ingredients and whisk to break up the eggs and combine. Cook over low heat, stirring contantly, with a heat safe rubber spatula until the mixture reaches 180°F (82°C). Remove from the heat and immediately strain into the bowl. Refrigerate. This will be a very loose cream.

STRAWBERRY SIMPLE SYRUP

120 g Soaking Syrup (page 198)

80 g strawberry puree

In a small bowl, combine the syrup with the puree. Set aside.

ITALIAN MERINGUE

400 g sugar, divided

90 g water

200 g egg whites

In a small saucepan, combine 350 grams of the sugar and the water and stir well. Place on the stove. Dip a pastry brush in a glass of water and then use it to wipe down any sugar crystals sticking to the insides of the pan above the sugar mixture. Place a thermometer in the mixture. Turn on the heat to medium and carefully watch the temperature. You will cook the sugar to a range of 245 to 250°F (118 to 121°C).

After you start cooking the sugar, place the egg whites in the bowl of the stand mixer fitted with the whisk attachment. When your sugar reaches 221°F (105°C), start whisking the egg whites on high speed. When they are foamy, stop the mixer, add the remaining 50 grams of sugar and then keep whisking on high speed. Now your goal is to bring the egg whites just to stiff peak at the same time as your sugar syrup reaches its temperature range. The most important thing to keep in mind is to not overcook the sugar or overwhip the egg whites. Err on the lower side, if necessary. To help sync the timing, you can always raise or lower your heat (or turn it off completely!) and raise or lower the speed at which you are whisking the eggs.

When your syrup reaches 245 to 250°F (118 to 121°C) and the egg whites are at stiff peak, reduce the mixer speed to low. Slowly pour the syrup down the side of the bowl and into the meringue, being careful not pour it on the whisk. Once all the syrup is in, continue to whisk the mixture on medium speed until the bottom of the bowl is no longer warm when you touch it, about 20 minutes. Use immediately (see Assembly, page 29).

ASSEMBLY

150 g fresh strawberries

Granulated sugar, for dusting

Slice 100 grams of the berries and reserve the rest for décor.

While the meringue is cooling in the mixer, lightly dust the top of the génoise with granulated sugar so it will not stick when unmolding. Cut around the edges to break the cake away from the sides of the pan. Place a piece of parchment over the cake and flip it upside down. Peel off the silicone mat slowly, starting at one corner and pulling the mat not up, but almost parallel to the mat itself in the opposite direction.

Cut out 5 circles from the cake with the following diameters: 20, 15, 13, 10 and 8 centimeters (8, 6, 5, 4 and 3 in). Be sure to start with the largest diameter and cut it as close to the edge as possible, so you can get all the sizes from one sheet of cake. Place the largest circle on a 25-centimeter (10-in) cake board or platter.

Warm the strawberry syrup. Soak the large cake circle with the syrup and then spread a layer of orange cream on top (about 200 grams). Place the sliced strawberries evenly on top of the cream.

Center the 15-centimeter (6-in) piece of cake on top of the strawberries. Soak with syrup and top with more cream (about 50 grams). Repeat with the rest of the cake layers, soaking and topping with cream. The layered cake should have a cone shape. Spread any remaining cream up the sides of the cone.

Place the Italian meringue in a piping bag fitted with a 2-centimeter (0.75-in) open plain tip. Pipe a curved line of meringue up the side of the cake, applying more pressure on the bag at the bottom, so it is thicker, and less as you reach the top, so it is thinner. Continue to do so until the whole cake is covered. Then, pipe a circle of dollops to create a nest on the top.

Using a propane torch, toast the meringue by passing the flame over the meringue in slow, even sweeps, going from bottom to top and then starting back at the bottom. Arrange the reserved strawberries in the top of the nest.

When piping the Italian meringue, apply more pressure to the pastry bag toward the bottom of the cake and less toward the top.

For torching meringue and créme brûlée, I recommend getting a propane torch from the hardware store, not a dinky culinary torch.

BÛCHE DE NOËL

DIFFICULTY: ● ● ◖

Can I get a ho, ho, ho?

A bûche de noël, or yule log cake, is found in almost every French household during Christmas-time in a variety of styles and flavors. Here is a more traditional style with a simple but delicious vanilla bean filling. We passed on the meringue mushrooms in favor of naughty pixies.

This chocolate biscuit cake contains only three ingredients and no flour. Be sure you do not overmix the meringue, or else it will fall apart when you are folding the batter together and your cake will not turn out as light as it should. For cocoa powder, choose an alkalized type for deep color and more chocolate flavor.

This buttercream is made with an Italian meringue. Italian meringue is the most difficult meringue but gives the lightest texture and thus is worth the effort. Have all your ingredients weighed and your equipment ready before starting.

YIELD: 9 servings

CHOCOLATE BISCUIT

120 g egg yolks

185 g egg whites

68 g sugar

50 g dark alkalized cocoa powder

Preheat the oven to 350°F (175°C). Line a half sheet pan with a silicone baking mat.

In the bowl of a stand mixer, whisk the egg yolks on high speed until they are thick and pale in color, about 5 minutes. Put the yolks into a bigger bowl with a larger surface area on top.

Prepare a French meringue (see page 191) with the egg whites and sugar, whisking to soft peak. Add half of the meringue to the yolks and gently fold to combine. Sift half of the cocoa onto the batter in a thin layer covering the top. Gently fold the cocoa into the batter. Repeat with the rest of the meringue and then the rest of the cocoa, being careful not to overmix. Ideally, if you have a helper in the kitchen, have the person continually sift the cocoa over the batter while you continually fold.

Spread evenly onto the half sheet pan, using an offset spatula. Bake until the cake is dry to the touch and feels firm, about 12 to 14 minutes.

VANILLA SOAKING SYRUP

125 g Soaking Syrup (page 198)

2.5 g (½ tsp) vanilla extract

In a small bowl, combine the syrup with the vanilla. Set aside.

VANILLA BEAN PASTRY CREAM

1 vanilla bean

500 g milk

100 g egg yolks

125 g sugar

40 g cornstarch

25 g unsalted butter, softened

Cut the vanilla bean in half lengthwise. Scrape out the seeds and place them in a small saucepan with the milk. Reserve the pod for décor. Bring the milk to a boil and then remove it from the heat.

In a medium bowl, combine the egg yolks, sugar and cornstarch and immediately whisk until the mixture turns pale, about 10 seconds. Slowly whisk the milk into the egg mixture and then strain it into a clean saucepan.

Over medium heat, whisk continually until the mixture starts to thicken, about 1 to 2 minutes. Pull off the heat and keep whisking while the mixture continues to thicken from the residual heat. Return the pan to the heat, still whisking, and cook until the mixture boils, being careful not to burn the bottom. Remove from the heat, add the butter and stir until it melts. Pour the pastry cream into a shallow bowl and place plastic wrap directly on top of the cream to prevent a skin from forming. Refrigerate immediately.

PARLOR TRICK! Make your pastry cream in the microwave! Place all the ingredients in a microwave-safe bowl. Blend them with an immersion blender and then place the bowl in the microwave. Cook on high until the top and sides of the pastry cream are set and jiggle like Jell-O when you shake the bowl, 5 to 7 minutes. The center will still be a bit liquid and the sides almost curdled. With a clean immersion blender, mix the pastry cream to combine, scrape the sides of the bowl and continue to blend in the center and also just at the surface until smooth. If, after blending, the cream is still very runny and has not thickened, continue to cook and blend until you have the consistency of pudding. Cover the surface with plastic wrap and refrigerate.

VANILLA BEAN BUTTERCREAM

1 vanilla bean

225 g sugar, divided

220 g water

68 g egg whites

225 g unsalted butter, softened

Cut the vanilla bean in half lengthwise and scrape the seeds into a small saucepan. Reserve the pod for décor. Add 170 grams of the sugar and the water and stir to combine. Place on the stove. Dip a pastry brush in a glass of water and then use it to wipe down any sugar crystals sticking to the insides of the pan above the water. Place a thermometer in the pan and turn on the heat to medium. Carefully watch the temperature. You will cook the sugar to a range of 245 to 250°F (118 to 121°C).

Place the egg whites in the bowl of a stand mixer fitted with the whisk attachment. When your sugar reaches 221°F (105°C), start whisking the egg whites on high speed. When they are foamy, add the remaining 55 grams of sugar and keep whisking. Now your goal is to bring the egg whites just to stiff peak at the same time your sugar syrup reaches its temperature range. The most important thing to keep in mind is to not overcook the sugar (it will be too hard to incorporate) or overwhip the egg whites (the meringue will collapse). Err on the lower side, if necessary. To help sync the timing, you can always raise or lower your heat (or turn it off completely!) and raise or lower the speed at which you are whisking the eggs.

When your syrup reaches 245 to 250°F (118 to 121°C) and the egg whites are at stiff peak, reduce the mixer speed to slow. *Slowly* pour the syrup down the side of the bowl and into the meringue, being careful not pour it on the whisk. Once all the syrup is in, continue to whisk the mixture on medium speed until the bottom of the bowl is no longer warm when you touch it, about 10 minutes. Add your softened butter and whisk on medium speed to combine, about 30 seconds. Use at room temperature. If the bottom of the whisk does not reach the egg whites in the bowl (for example, if you have a 5.7 L [6 qt] bowl or larger) you can use a towel to prop up one side. Place the towel on the arm of the stand mixer with the bowl resting on top of the towel but still secure to the stand mixer in the back. Do this with the mixer turned off.

Pull on the parchment to roll the cake into a tight cylinder.

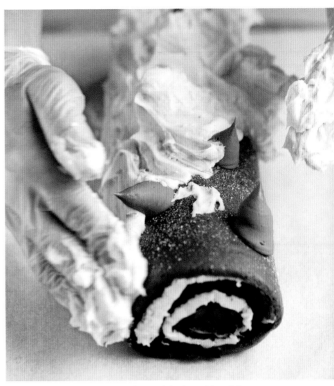

Slather the branches, sides and top of the log with soft buttercream.

Make a barklike pattern in the buttercream with your fingers.

Use a warm knife to cut the buttercream stubs and reveal the "branches."

ASSEMBLY

Granulated sugar, for dusting

40 g dark chocolate

Fresh rosemary, as desired

Pixies, as desired

Lightly dust the cake top with granulated sugar, so it will not stick when unmolding. Cut around the edges to break the cake away from the sides of the pan. Place a piece of parchment over the cake and flip it upside down. Peel off the silicone mat slowly, starting at one corner and pulling the mat not up, but almost parallel to the mat itself in the opposite direction.

Slide the cake, still upside down and on the parchment, onto a half sheet pan. Turn the pan so the shorter side faces you. On the side farthest from you, pull out the parchment from under the cake by about 2.5 centimeters (1 in). This will help you roll the cake later.

In a small saucepan, heat the vanilla syrup until hot. Using a pastry brush, soak the cake generously with the syrup. Place the pastry cream in the bowl of a stand mixer fitted with the paddle attachment and beat it on high speed until smooth, about 30 seconds. Spread the pastry cream evenly over the cake. Chill it in the freezer for about 30 minutes. You want the cream to be fairly firm but not completely frozen and the cake still flexible. Chilling the cake will make it easier to handle and roll.

Place the cake in front of you with the parchment edge farthest away. Use the parchment paper to help you lift up the cake edge and fold 2.5 centimeters (1 in) over onto itself. Then, pull up on the parchment and use it to roll the cake toward you, trying to keep the cylinder as tight and round as possible. Place the cake back in the freezer for 1 hour.

Melt the dark chocolate. Add 60 grams of the buttercream and mix with a rubber spatula. Place the mixture in a piping bag fitted with a medium-size round tip. Pipe knobs of cream in a random pattern along the log to represent the wood of the branches. Place in the refrigerator to chill until the cream is hardened, about 10 minutes. Meanwhile, place your buttercream in the clean bowl of the stand mixer and soften it by beating on high speed with the paddle attachment for 3 minutes. The buttercream should not be cold at all. If the bottom of the bowl is at all cold, you can use a torch to warm the bowl and thus the buttercream.

Remove the log from the refrigerator and place on a clean piece of parchment paper. Using your hands, slather the branches, top and sides of the log with the buttercream, making a barklike pattern as you go. Next, trim the tops of the branches in random directions with a warm paring knife, to reveal the "wood." A torch works nicely for warming the knife. Otherwise, you can use hot water. Be sure to wipe the blade after every cut. Finally, trim the log ends at an angle to get a flat surface on each end. Decorate with the vanilla bean pods, rosemary sprigs and some naughty pixies.

CHAPTER TWO

TARTS

The beautiful thing about a tart is the crunch the shell lends to the dessert. This chapter shares three different tart doughs.

SWEET TART DOUGH—Also known as pâte sucrée in French. This dough is the sweetest of the three, buttery and very crunchy.

ALMOND TART DOUGH—This dough is less sweet and more crumbly (versus crunchy) than the Sweet Tart Dough. The almonds lend a nice richness to the dough.

CHOCOLATE ALMOND TART DOUGH—Similar in texture to the Almond Tart Dough but with a pleasant bitter note from the cocoa that balances the sugar content.

Feel free to interchange them in recipes. You can also make the large tarts into an individual serving size and individual tart recipes into large tarts for sharing. Straight-sided tart rings are preferred for their simplicity and uniformity, but you can also use fluted tart shell molds.

A MOMENT OF ZEN

DIFFICULTY: 🍪 🍪 🍪

Beautiful things can bring a sense of peace and pause. Let this dessert help share that.

This tart is a celebration of "fruits rouges" (red fruits), featuring a raspberry mousse, blackberry coulis, black currant pastry cream and whatever your fancy for the fruit décor. Sure to be a show-stopper . . . it got your attention, no? Seek out a high-quality crème de cassis (black currant liqueur) from a local wine shop.

For this recipe we used a Silikomart "Yin Yang" paisley-shaped mold and a 28-centimeter (11-in) tart ring (see Sources on page 199). Alternatively, you can mold the mousse in a 20-centimeter (8 in) cake ring lined with acetate. You will also need a 20-centimeter (8-in) cake ring for the blackberry coulis.

YIELD: 12 servings

SWEET TART DOUGH

100 g egg yolks

5 g (1 tsp) vanilla extract

310 g all-purpose flour, plus more for rolling and baking

Pinch of salt

140 g powdered sugar

240 g unsalted butter, cold

In a small bowl, whisk together the egg yolks and vanilla and set aside. Sift the flour, salt and sugar into the bowl of a stand mixer fitted with the paddle attachment and combine on low speed. Cut the butter into 1-centimeter (0.5-in) cubes and add to the flour mixture. Continue to mix on low speed until the mixture resembles coarse sand, about 5 minutes. Do not overmix. If the mixture starts to stick together, it will not absorb the eggs and it will be very sticky and hard to roll. Add the egg yolk mixture and mix just until incorporated and you have a homogenous dough, about 30 seconds. Form the dough into a flattened circle and wrap it in plastic wrap. Refrigerate for 1 hour, minimum.

RASPBERRY MOUSSE

13 g powdered gelatin

65 g cold water

385 g raspberry puree

190 g powdered sugar

385 g heavy cream

In a medium, microwave-safe bowl, combine the gelatin with the cold water and stir well to dissolve. Let sit for 5 minutes to bloom.

Place the puree in a medium saucepan. Sift the powdered sugar and whisk it into the puree. Heat the puree over medium heat until slightly warm, about 2 minutes.

Place the cream in the bowl of the stand mixer fitted with the whisk attachment and whisk to soft peak.

Melt the gelatin on low in the microwave. Swirl the bowl to stir the gelatin every 30 seconds, until it is completely melted. Whisking constantly by hand, slowly add one-third of the slightly warm puree to the gelatin. Add the remaining puree and whisk to combine. Add half of the puree to the cream and fold with a whisk, followed by the second half. Pour into the paisley mold and freeze overnight.

RASPBERRY MIRROR

7 g powdered gelatin

35 g cold water

140 g Soaking Syrup (page 198)

140 g raspberry puree

In a medium bowl, combine the gelatin with the cold water and stir well to dissolve. Let sit for 5 minutes to bloom.

In a small saucepan, heat the soaking syrup until warm. Add the gelatin and stir until melted. Slowly stir in the puree. Refrigerate.

BLACKBERRY COULIS

5 g powdered gelatin

25 g cold water

190 g blackberry puree

60 g sugar

Place a 20-centimeter (8-in) cake ring on a half sheet pan lined with parchment. Pull the parchment up the outer sides of the ring and secure it with a large rubber band.

In a small bowl, combine the gelatin with the cold water and stir well to dissolve. Let sit for 5 minutes to bloom.

In a small saucepan, combine the puree and sugar and cook over medium heat just until warm and the sugar is dissolved, about 2 minutes. Add the solid gelatin mass to the puree and stir until the gelatin is melted. Pour into the cake ring. Freeze for at least 4 hours.

CRÈME DE CASSIS PASTRY CREAM

400 g milk

80 g egg yolks

100 g sugar

32 g cornstarch

20 g unsalted butter

30 g crème de cassis

5 g (1 tsp) fresh lime juice

In a microwave-safe bowl, combine all the pastry cream ingredients, except the crème de cassis and lime juice. Blend them with an immersion blender and then place the bowl in the microwave. Cook on high until the top and sides of the pastry cream are set and jiggle like Jell-O when you shake the bowl, 5 to 7 minutes. The center will still be a bit liquid and the sides almost curdled. With a clean immersion blender, mix the pastry cream to combine, scrape the sides of the bowl and continue to blend in the center and also just at the surface until smooth. If, after blending, the cream is still very runny and has not thickened, continue to cook and blend until you have the consistency of pudding. Cover the surface with plastic wrap and refrigerate.

When ready to use, transfer the pastry cream to the bowl of a stand mixer fitted with the paddle attachment and beat until smooth, about 30 seconds. Add the crème de cassis and lime juice and stir to combine.

ASSEMBLY

Plums, pitted, as needed

Edible flowers

DÉCOR

Watermelon, as needed

Blackberries, as needed

Raspberries, as needed

Blueberries, as needed

Strawberries, as needed

Preheat the oven to 350°F (175°C). Roll out the tart dough to a thickness of 0.5 centimeter (0.2 in). Line a 28-centimeter (11-in) tart shell or ring with the dough and chill for at least 20 minutes. Before baking, weigh the dough down with flour wrapped in plastic wrap (see Techniques, page 195).

Bake until the edges look set, 20 to 22 minutes. Remove the plastic and continue to bake until the bottom of the tart is light golden brown, about 10 to 12 minutes. Allow to cool.

Spread half of the pastry cream in the tart shell. Unmold the frozen blackberry coulis and place it in the center. Top with the remaining pastry cream.

Heat the raspberry mirror to 86°F (30°C), stirring carefully so as not to introduce any air bubbles. Unmold the frozen raspberry mousse and place it on a wire rack over a half sheet pan. Pour the mirror over the mousse to cover all sides and let sit for 1 minute. Using a large offset spatula, lift the mousse off the rack and position it in the upper left-hand corner of the tart shell. Decorate the other half with the fresh fruit and flowers.

THE OREGON GET DOWN

DIFFICULTY:

Get down, and get on up. This is gonna make you wanna dance!

Living in Oregon, it's hard not to fall in love with our beautiful hazelnuts and juicy pears, which just happen to pair lovely together. They also pair perfectly with rosemary, which is used here to infuse a silky, milk chocolate ganache. (You may even want to make an extra batch and stir some into your morning latte. Yes, you do. Trust me.)

Choose pears that are not too soft but still ripe with bold flavor, such as Bosc. If buying at the grocery store, shop a couple days ahead and allow the pears to ripen on the kitchen counter. For this recipe, you will need a 20-centimeter (8-in) tart ring, plus a 15-centimeter (6-in) cake ring and 5 centimeter (2-in) cutter for the décor.

YIELD: 10 servings

SWEET TART DOUGH

50 g egg yolks

2.5 g (½ tsp) vanilla extract

155 g all-purpose flour, plus more for rolling and baking

Pinch of salt

70 g powdered sugar

120 g unsalted butter, cold

In a medium bowl, whisk together the egg yolks and vanilla and set aside. Sift the flour, salt and sugar into the bowl of a stand mixer fitted with the paddle attachment and combine on low speed. Cut the butter into 1-centimeter (0.5-in) cubes and add to the flour mixture. Continue to mix on low speed until the mixture resembles coarse sand, about 5 minutes. Do not overmix. If the mixture starts to stick together, it will not absorb the eggs and it will be very sticky and hard to roll. Add the egg yolk mixture and mix just until incorporated and you have a homogenous dough, about 30 seconds. Form the dough into a flattened circle and wrap it in plastic wrap. Refrigerate for 1 hour, minimum.

CARAMELIZED PEARS

1 pear

100 g sugar

30 g pear brandy

Peel the pear and cut it into 1.5-centimeter (0.5-in) cubes, discarding the center seeds and stems. Place the sugar in a medium sauce pan over medium heat. Cook the sugar to melt and then caramelize (see Techniques, page 190). Lower the heat, add the pears, stir and cover with a lid. Allow the pears to simmer until partially softened, about 5 minutes.

Remove the lid. Add the pear brandy and carefully ignite the alcohol by taking a match to the edge of the pan. Cook until the flame extinguishes itself, about 20 seconds. Remove from the heat.

HAZELNUT CREAM

60 g unsalted butter

60 g brown sugar

5 g (1 tsp) vanilla extract

50 g eggs

60 g hazelnut meal

12 g pastry flour

Place the butter and brown sugar in the bowl of a stand mixer fitted with the paddle attachment. Mix on medium speed until incorporated and lighter in texture, about 2 minutes, scraping down the sides of the bowl as needed. Add the vanilla and half of the eggs and continue to mix, scraping down the sides of the bowl as needed, until combined. Add the rest of the eggs and repeat. Add the hazelnut meal and the flour. Mix on low speed just until combined, about 30 seconds.

ROSEMARY GANACHE

100 g heavy cream

5 g fresh rosemary

125 g milk chocolate

Pinch of salt

In a small saucepan, bring the cream to a boil. Remove it from the heat and add the rosemary. Cover and infuse for 15 minutes. Meanwhile, in a microwave-safe bowl, melt the milk chocolate in the microwave on low, stirring often. Strain the cream and discard the rosemary. Add the infused cream and salt to the chocolate and whisk until smooth. Use immediately (see Assembly, page 45).

DÉCOR

20 g hazelnuts

115 g nougatine (page 189)

> **PARLOR TRICK!** Should the cooled nougatine décor break, you can place it back in the food processor and start again.

Preheat the oven to 300°F (150°C). Line a half sheet pan with a silicone baking mat.

Toast the hazelnuts in the oven, about 10 minutes, and remove their skins by rubbing the nuts against the inside of a strainer. Set aside.

Grind the nougatine to a fine powder in a food processor. Place a 15-centimeter (6-in) cake ring on the baking mat. Sift the nougatine powder over the ring to evenly cover the bottom inside. Place a 5-centimeter (2-in) circle pastry cutter inside the ring in the upper left side. Bake until the caramel starts to melt and the nougatine powder sticks together, 8 to 10 minutes. Remove the pan from the oven and then remove the rings from the pan. Allow the nougatine to cool and harden.

 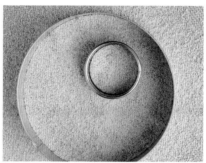 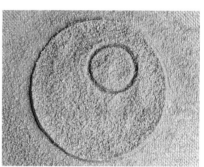

ASSEMBLY

Fresh rosemary, as desired

Preheat the oven to 350°F (175°C). Roll out the tart dough to a thickness of 0.5 centimeters (0.2 in). Line a 20-centimeter (8-in) tart shell or ring with the dough and chill for at least 20 minutes. Before baking, weigh the dough down with flour wrapped in plastic wrap (see Techniques, page 195).

Bake until the edges look set, about 15 minutes. Remove the plastic and continue to bake until the bottom of the tart is dry to the touch and barely starting to brown, about 10 minutes. Add the hazelnut cream in spoonfuls over the bottom of the tart. Return to the oven for 2 minutes to allow the cream to partially melt. Remove from the oven and spread the cream to cover the entire bottom of the tart. Strain the pears and sprinkle them over the cream. Return to the oven and bake until the almond cream is set and dry, 16 to 18 minutes. Cool completely.

Pour the rosemary ganache over the hazelnut cream to fill the tart shell. Chill in the refrigerator until set, about 30 minutes.

Reserve about 5 hazelnuts and space out the rest on top of the ganache. Gently slide a small offset spatula under the edges of the nougatine décor to release it from the mat.

Place the décor on top of the hazelnuts so it looks like it's floating. Arrange the remaining hazelnuts sporadically to the top of the nougatine. Garnish the circle with fresh-cut rosemary.

SOLEIL

DIFFICULTY:

You might need sunscreen, FYI.

This brilliantly colored tart will make any day seem like summer. With its mango rays, creamy center with a burst of pineapple and crunchy shell, it's like going on vacation everytime you eat it. Star anise in the pastry cream adds another yet subtle dimension of flavor. Fresh pineapple is preferred, but make sure it is ripe. I usually buy my pineapple three days in advance and let it ripen on the counter.

For this recipe, you will need a 20-centimeter (8-in) tart ring and a 15-centimeter (6-in) disk-shaped silicone mold or cake ring for the mango cream.

YIELD: 10 servings

SWEET TART DOUGH

50 g egg yolks

2.5 g (½ tsp) vanilla extract

155 g all-purpose flour, plus more for rolling and baking

Pinch of salt

70 g powdered sugar

120 g unsalted butter, cold

In a medium bowl, whisk together the egg yolks and vanilla and set aside. Sift the flour, salt and sugar into the bowl of a stand mixer fitted with the paddle attachment and combine on low speed. Cut the butter into 1-centimeter (0.5-in) cubes and add to the bowl. Continue to mix on low speed until the mixture resembles coarse sand, about 5 minutes. Do not overmix. If the mixture starts to stick together, it will not absorb the eggs and it will be very sticky and hard to roll. Add the egg yolk mixture and mix just until incorporated and you have a homogenous dough, about 30 seconds. Form the dough into a flattened circle and wrap it in plastic wrap. Refrigerate for 1 hour, minimum.

MANGO CREAM

3 g powdered gelatin

15 g cold water

140 g mango puree

40 g egg yolks

50 g sugar

50 g unsalted butter

Place a 15-centimeter (6-in) disk-shaped silicone mold or cake ring lined with acetate on a half sheet pan. If using the ring, line the half sheet with parchment.

In a small bowl, combine the gelatin with the cold water and stir well to dissolve. Let sit for 5 minutes to bloom.

Place a strainer over a medium bowl, next to the stove. In a small saucepan, combine the mango puree, yolks and sugar. Cook over low heat, stirring constantly with a heat-safe rubber spatula and making sure the mixture does not stick to the bottom or corners of the pan. Right when the mixture reaches 180°F (82°C), immediately strain it into the bowl. Add the butter and the gelatin mixture and stir to melt. Pour into the mold. Freeze for at least 4 hours.

ANISE PASTRY CREAM

300 g milk

2 star anise

60 g egg yolks

24 g cornstarch

75 g sugar

15 g unsalted butter

In a medium saucepan, bring the milk to a boil. Remove from the heat and add the star anise. Cover and infuse for 15 minutes. Pull out the star anise, wash it and save it for décor.

In a medium bowl, combine the egg yolks, cornstarch and sugar and immediately whisk until the mixture turns pale. Slowly whisk the milk into the egg mixture and then strain it into a clean saucepan.

Over medium heat, whisk constantly until the mixture starts to thicken, about 1 to 2 minutes. Pull off the heat and keep whisking while the mixture continues to thicken from the residual heat. Return the pan to the heat, still whisking, until the mixture boils, being careful not to burn the bottom. Remove from the heat, add the butter and stir until it melts. Pour the pastry cream into a bowl and place plastic wrap directly on top of the cream to prevent a skin from forming. Refrigerate immediately.

PINEAPPLE FILLING

1 vanilla bean

150 g Soaking Syrup (page 198)

200 g pineapple

Cut the vanilla bean in half lengthwise. Scrape out the seeds and place them and the pod in a small saucepan along with the soaking syrup. Chop the pineapple into small tidbits and add it to the saucepan. Simmer for 20 minutes, stirring occasionally. Refrigerate.

ASSEMBLY

2 mangoes

Preheat the oven to 350°F (175°C).

Roll out the tart dough to a thickness of 0.5 centimeter (0.2 in). Line a 20-centimeter (8-in) tart shell or ring with the dough and chill for at least 20 minutes. Before baking, weigh the dough down with flour wrapped in plastic wrap (see Techniques, page 195).

Bake until the edges look set, about 18 minutes. Remove the plastic and continue to bake until the bottom of the tart is light golden brown, about 10 minutes. Allow to cool.

Place the pastry cream in the bowl of the stand mixer fitted with the paddle attachment and beat to soften. Spread three-fourths of the pastry cream in the bottom of the tart shell. Strain the pineapple, saving the vanilla bean pod for décor. Spread the pineapple on top of the pastry cream in an even layer.

Locate the pit of each mango and cut a large section off along both sides. With the flat portion of the mango sections face down, peel each mango with a paring knife, trying to keep a smooth curvature along the top. Cut the sections into 0.5-centimeter (0.2-in)-thick slices and arrange them around the edge of the tart. Add the remaining quarter of pastry cream to the tart and smooth it with a small offset spatula, making the top as flat as possible. Unmold the frozen mango cream and place it in the center, covering the inside edges of the mango slices. Decorate with star anise and the vanilla bean pod. Serve the same day as assembled.

Cut a large section of fruit off both sides of the mango pit.

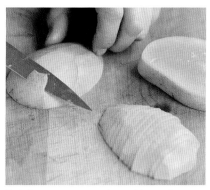
Peel the cut mango sections with a paring knife.

Cut the mango sections into thin slices.

GOING BANANAS

DIFFICULTY:

That's just where your guests will be going when they taste this tart. Bananas.

A surprise element of yellow curry will really grab their attention, and their taste buds, when they reach the center. The crème chiboust is a classic French cream made by combining pastry cream, meringue and gelatin. Torch it with a flame not to create a hard crack shell like on crème brûlée, but just enough to give it a toasty flavor like marshmallows in a campfire.

For this recipe, you will need a 20-centimeter (8-in) tart ring.

YIELD: 10 servings

CHOCOLATE TART DOUGH

68 g powdered sugar

18 g cocoa powder

150 g all-purpose flour, plus more for rolling and baking

22 g almond meal

2.5 g (½ tsp) salt

90 g unsalted butter, cold

50 g eggs

Sift the sugar, cocoa and flour into the bowl of a stand mixer fitted with the paddle attachment. Add the almond meal and salt. Stir to combine. Cut the butter into 1-centimeter (0.5-in) cubes and add to the bowl. Mix on low speed until the mixture resembles coarse sand, about 5 minutes. Add the eggs and mix just until the dough starts to stick together, about 2 minutes. Do not overmix. Form the dough into a flattened circle and wrap it in plastic wrap. Refrigerate for 1 hour, minimum.

PASTRY CREAM

250 g milk

50 g egg yolks

20 g cornstarch

62 g sugar

12 g unsalted butter

Place all the pastry cream ingredients in a microwave-safe bowl. Blend them with an immersion blender and then place the bowl in the microwave. Cook on high until the top and sides of the pastry cream are set and jiggle like Jell-O when you shake the bowl, about 3 minutes. The center will still be a bit liquid and the sides almost curdled. With a clean immersion blender, mix the pastry cream to combine, scrape the sides of the bowl and continue to blend in the center and also just at the surface until smooth. If, after blending, the cream is still very runny and has not thickened, continue to cook and blend until you have the consistency of pudding. Cover the surface with plastic wrap and refrigerate.

CURRIED BANANAS FLAMBÉ

200 g (about 2 medium) bananas

25 g unsalted butter

65 g brown sugar

8 g (1 tbsp) curry powder

35 g dark rum

Slice the bananas into 1-centimeter (0.5-in) medallions. In a medium-wide skillet over medium heat, melt the butter. In a small bowl, stir the brown sugar and curry together and add them to the skillet. Stir until the brown sugar dissolves into the butter and the mixture starts to bubble around the edges. Add the banana slices and stir to coat them completely with the sugar mixture. Cook undisturbed for 2 minutes.

At arm's length from the stove, add the rum quickly and give the pan a quick shake to spread it out. If the mixture does not flame up on its own, take a lit match to the edge of the pan to ignite the rum. Continue to cook for 30 seconds. The flame will extinguish itself. Remove from the heat and transfer to a clean bowl.

CRÈME CHIBOUST

2 g powdered gelatin

10 g cold water

125 g milk

25 g egg yolks

57 g sugar, divided, plus more for sprinkling

10 g cornstarch

12 g unsalted butter, softened

60 g egg whites

Prepare after baking the tart dough (see Assembly).

In a small bowl, combine the gelatin with the cold water and stir well to dissolve. Let sit for 5 minutes to bloom.

In a microwave-safe bowl, combine the milk, egg yolks, 32 grams of the sugar, cornstarch and butter. Blend with an immersion blender and then place the bowl in the microwave. Cook on high until the top and sides of the milk mixture are set and jiggle like Jell-O when you shake the bowl, about 1½ minutes. The center will still be a bit liquid and the sides almost curdled. With a clean immersion blender, mix the milk mixture to combine, scrape the sides of the bowl and continue to blend in the center and also just at the surface until smooth. If, after blending, the cream is still very runny and has not thickened, continue to cook and blend until you have the consistency of pudding. Add the gelatin mixture and stir to melt.

Prepare a French meringue (see page 198) with the egg whites and remaining 25 grams of sugar, whisking to stiff peak.

When the milk mixture has cooled to 104°F (40°C), fold half of the meringue into it, using a whisk. Once incorporated, fold in the second half. Use immediately.

ASSEMBLY

Sugar

1 banana

Chocolate curls (see Techniques, page 190), as desired

Gold leaf, as desired

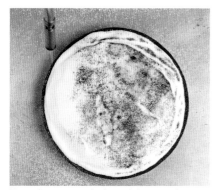

Toast the sugar and crème chiboust with a torch.

Preheat the oven to 350°F (175°C). Roll out the chocolate tart dough to a thickness of 0.5 centimeter (0.2 in) and a diameter of about 25 centimeters (10 in). Line a 20-centimeter (8-in) tart shell or ring with the dough and chill for at least 20 minutes. Before baking, weigh the dough down with flour wrapped in plastic wrap (see Techniques, page 195).

Bake until the edges look set, about 15 minutes. Remove the plastic and continue to bake until the bottom of the tart is dry to the touch, 10 to 12 minutes. When pressed with your finger, it should not be oily. Allow to cool completely.

Lower the oven to 325°F (160°C). Place the cooled pastry cream into the bowl of a stand mixer fitted with the paddle attachment. Beat on high until smooth, about 30 seconds. Stir in the bananas. Place this mixture into the baked tart shell, still in the ring. Return to the oven and bake for 30 minutes. When removed from the oven, the filling will be a little loose in the center. Chill the tart.

Prepare the crème chiboust. Pile the chiboust onto the top of the tart and smooth it with an offset spatula. Refrigerate for at least 20 minutes.

Sprinkle the top of the crème chiboust with an even, thin layer of sugar. Toast the sugar with a propane torch, using the lowest setting. The top will resemble toasted marshmallow rather than crème brûlée. Decorate with one-third of a banana, chocolate curls and gold leaf.

STRAWBERRY FIELDS

DIFFICULTY: 🍪

Well, less of a field and more like a raised bed. Delicious nonetheless.

Ideally you'll want to make this tart when strawberry season is at its peak and the
berries are juicy and bursting with flavor. Return to the stawberry patch for a picnic and
enjoy it with a bottle of rosé champagne.

The tart was baked in a 20-centimeter (8-in) square tart ring but you can substutute a circle ring.
Bake the tart shell and make the "grass" a day in advance so it has time to dry.

YIELD: 8 servings

SWEET TART DOUGH

50 g egg yolks

2.5 g (½ tsp) vanilla extract

155 g all-purpose flour, plus more for
rolling and baking

Pinch of salt

70 g powdered sugar

120 g unsalted butter, cold

In a small bowl, whisk together the egg yolks and vanilla and set aside. Sift the flour,
salt and sugar into the bowl of a stand mixer fitted with the paddle attachment and
combine on low speed. Cut the butter into 1-centimeter (0.5-in) cubes and add to the
bowl. Continue to mix on low speed until the mixture resembles coarse sand, about
5 minutes. Do not overmix. If the mixture starts to stick together, it will not absorb
the eggs and it will be very sticky and hard to roll. Add the egg yolk mixture and mix
just until incorporated and you have a homogenous dough, about 30 seconds. Form
the dough into a flattened circle and wrap it in plastic wrap. Refrigerate for 1 hour,
minimum.

STRAWBERRY COULIS

3 g powdered gelatin

15 g cold water

75 g strawberries

85 g strawberry puree

15 g fresh lime juice

45 g sugar

In a small bowl, combine the gelatin with the cold water and stir well to dissolve. Let sit for 5 minutes to bloom. Chop the strawberries into 0.5-centimeter (0.2-in) pieces and place in a small bowl.

In a small saucepan, combine the puree, lime juice and sugar and heat just until warm and the sugar is dissolved. Add the solid gelatin mass to the puree and stir until the gelatin is melted, then pour the mixture into the bowl of strawberries. Refrigerate.

BASIL PASTRY CREAM

300 g milk

4 g fresh basil

60 g egg yolks

75 g sugar

24 g cornstarch

15 g unsalted butter

In a small saucepan, bring the milk to a boil. Remove from the heat and add the basil. Cover and infuse for 15 minutes. Strain the milk and discard the basil.

In a medium bowl, combine the egg yolks, sugar and cornstarch and immediately whisk until the mixture turns pale, about 10 seconds. Slowly whisk the milk into the egg mixture and then pour it into a clean saucepan.

Over medium heat, whisk constantly until the mixture starts to thicken, about 1 to 2 minutes. Pull off the heat and keep whisking while the mixture continues to thicken from the residual heat. Return the pan to the heat, still whisking, until the mixture boils, being careful not to burn the bottom. Remove from the heat, add the butter and stir until it melts. Pour the pastry cream into a bowl and place plastic wrap directly on top of the cream to prevent a skin from forming. Refrigerate immediately.

BASIL GRASS

75 g sweet tart dough

10 g basil

Bake the tart dough scraps (see Assembly). Place the crumbs and basil in a food processor and process. Spread out on a sheet pan and allow to dry overnight. Push the crumbs through a fine sieve to break them apart.

ASSEMBLY

12 strawberries

Preheat the oven to 350°F (175°C).

Roll out the tart dough to a thickness of 0.5 centimeters (0.2 in). Line a 20-centimeter (8-in) square tart shell or ring with the dough and chill for at least 20 minutes. Before baking, weigh the dough down with flour wrapped in plastic wrap (see Techniques, page 195). Take the scraps from rolling and chill those on a second sheet pan lined with a silicone baking mat.

Bake the tart until the edges look set, about 18 minutes. Remove the plastic and continue to bake until the bottom of the tart is light golden brown, about 10 minutes. Bake the dough scraps in the same oven at the same time but remove them earlier, just when their edges just start to brown, about 15 minutes. Allow both to cool.

In the bowl of the stand mixer fitted with the paddle attachment, beat the pastry cream to soften, about 20 seconds. Spread the strawberry coulis evenly over the bottom of the tart. Spread the pastry over the coulis to cover completely.

Sift the "grass" over the tart until all the cream is covered. Top with the whole strawberries.

CONCERTO

DIFFICULTY: 🍪 🍪

A whimsical composition of coffee, caramel and peanuts. Fleur de sel plays the solo.

I love this dessert for its array of textures and its contrasting sweet and salty flavors. Creamy, coffee mousse; sticky, sweet caramel; crunchy, salty peanuts—all packed together in a bittersweet chocolate shell. Music to my mouth.

For this recipe, you will need two silicone disk molds of 6 centimeters (2.4 in) in diameter with 8 cavities per mold and 12 tart rings or molds approximately 8 centimeters (3.2 in) in diameter and preferably 2.5 centimeters (1 in) in height.

YIELD: 12 individual tarts

COFFEE CREAM

15 g coffee beans

180 g milk

4 g powdered gelatin

20 g cold water

60 g egg yolks

44 g sugar

150 g heavy cream

Place 2 (6 centimeter [2.4 in])-diameter silicone disk molds on a half sheet pan.

Lightly crush the coffee beans in a plastic bag, using a rolling pin. In a small saucepan, bring the milk to a boil, remove it from the heat and add the coffee beans. Cover and infuse for 15 minutes. Strain and discard the beans.

In a small bowl, combine the gelatin with the cold water and stir well to dissolve. Let sit for 5 minutes to bloom.

In a small bowl, whisk together the egg yolks and sugar until pale, about 30 seconds. Slowly add the milk while whisking. Transfer the mixture to a medium saucepan with a thermometer. Place a strainer over a clean bowl, next to the stove. Cook the mixture over low heat, stirring constantly with a heat-safe rubber spatula. When the mixture reaches 180°F (82°C), immediately strain it into the bowl. Add the gelatin and stir until melted. Allow to cool at room temperature, scraping the bowl down and stirring often so the gelatin sets up evenly. Once cool, blend briefly with an immersion blender to make sure there are no lumps.

In the bowl of the stand mixer fitted with the whisk attachment, whisk the cream to stiff peak. Remove one-fourth of the whipped cream and whisk it quickly into the coffee mixture. Then pour the coffee mixture into the remaining whipped cream and fold with the whisk until combined. Pour the coffee cream into the molds. Freeze overnight.

FLEUR DE SEL CARAMEL

260 g heavy cream

1 vanilla bean

340 g sugar

32 g unsalted butter

3.5 g (¾ tsp) fleur de sel sea salt

In a small saucepan, bring the cream to a simmer and set aside.

Cut the vanilla bean in half lengthwise. Scrape out the seeds and place them and the pod in a large saucepan. Add one-fourth of the sugar to the vanilla and cook over medium heat. When you see the edges of the sugar start to melt, after about 1 minute, stir briefly with a wooden spoon and allow the edges to melt again. Stir again and repeat until all the sugar is melted, about another minute. It will have a light, opaque caramel color. Add the rest of the sugar, one-fourth at a time, and follow the same procedure.

Right when you have a deep caramel color, add the hot cream, little by little, batting the rising foam back and forth with your spoon until it subsides. Then, add more cream. Strain into a small bowl. Add the butter and stir to melt. Stir in the fleur de sel and allow to cool.

COFFEE CARAMEL GLAZE

20 g coffee beans

300 g heavy cream

8 g powdered gelatin

40 g cold water

140 g sugar

Roughly crush the coffee beans in a plastic bag, using a rolling pin. In a small saucepan, bring the cream to a boil, remove it from the heat and add the coffee beans. Cover and infuse for 15 minutes. Strain and discard the beans.

In a small bowl, combine the gelatin with the cold water and stir well to dissolve. Let sit for 5 minutes to bloom.

In a large saucepan, caramelize the sugar, adding one-fourth at a time to the pan, as you did in making the fleur de sel caramel. Meanwhile, bring the cream back to a simmer. When the sugar is melted and deep caramel in color, slowly add the cream while stirring. Strain into a bowl, add the gelatin and stir to melt. Reserve at room temperature.

PHYLLO DÉCOR

35 g unsalted butter

2 (33 x 46 cm [13 x 18 in]) sheets phyllo dough

Sugar, as needed

Preheat the oven to 350°F (175°C). Line a half sheet pan with a silicone baking mat.

Carefully melt the butter so it is warm but not hot. Place a sheet of phyllo on a piece of parchment. Brush one side of the phyllo entirely with butter. Sprinkle generously with the sugar. Cut the sheet into thirds and then halves, so you have 6 pieces total. Crumble a piece gently into a loose wad (like a used napkin!) and place them on the pan. Repeat with the second sheet of phyllo for 12 pieces total. Bake until the phyllo seems firm to the touch, about 8 minutes.

CHOCOLATE ALMOND DOUGH

135 g powdered sugar

35 g dark alkalized cocoa powder

300 g all-purpose flour, plus more for
rolling and baking

45 g almond meal

5 g (1 tsp) salt

180 g unsalted butter, cold

100 g eggs

Sift the sugar, cocoa and flour into the bowl of a stand mixer fitted with the paddle attachment. Add the almond meal and salt. Stir to combine. Cut the butter into 1-centimeter (0.5 in) cubes and add to the bowl. Mix on low speed until the mixture resembles coarse sand, about 5 minutes. Add the eggs and mix just until the dough starts to stick together, about 2 minutes. Do not overmix. Form the dough into a flattened circle and wrap it in plastic wrap. Refrigerate for 1 hour, minimum.

ASSEMBLY

150 g peanuts, roasted and salted

DÉCOR POWDER

20 g dark alkalized cocoa powder

2 g (1 tsp) gold dust

Preheat the oven to 350°F (175°C).

Roll out the dough to a thickness of 0.5 centimeters (0.2 in). Line twelve 8 centimeter (3.2 in) diameter tart shells or rings with the dough and chill for at least 20 minutes. Before baking, weigh the dough down with flour wrapped in plastic wrap (see Techniques, page 195).

Bake until the edges look set, about 10 minutes. Remove the plastic and continue to bake until the bottom of the tart is dry to the touch, about 10 minutes. When pressed with your finger, it should not be oily. Allow to cool.

Add about 12 grams of peanuts to each baked tart shell. Warm the caramel slightly to pouring consistency, if necessary. Cover the peanuts with caramel, leaving about a space of 0.5 centimeter (0.2 in) between the caramel and the top edge of the tart. Chill for 15 minutes to firm up the caramel.

Unmold the frozen coffee cream disks and place them on a wire rack with a sheet of parchment underneath to catch drips. Warm the caramel glaze to 86°F (30°C) and pour it over the coffee cream. If more glaze is needed, the runoff glaze on the parchment can be reheated and used again. Using an offset spatula, lift the coffee cream just above the rack and rub the edges on the rack in a circular motion to remove any excess glaze. Position the coffee cream in the center of the tart shell. Lightly sprinkle décor powder over the phyllo. Top each tart with a piece of the phyllo.

SUNSET ON
THE BOULEVARD

DIFFICULTY: 🍪 🍪

Let's take a Sunday drive.

This tart comingles rich, creamy lavender crème brûlée with the racy citrus notes of
grapefruit mousse. The texture is further bolstered with a bed of soft almond cream
and a crunchy, almond tart shell.

For this recipe, you will need a 20-centimeter (8-in) tart ring and two 15-cavity silicone dome
molds, each 4 centimeters (1.5 in). You can make the recipe with one dome mold by allowing the
crème brûlée to freeze and unmold before making the grapefruit mousse.

YIELD: 10 servings

ALMOND TART DOUGH

100 g unsalted butter, softened

50 g powdered sugar

1 g (⅛ tsp) salt

40 g almond meal

60 g egg yolks

2.5 g (½ tsp) vanilla extract

165 g all-purpose flour

Place the butter, sugar, salt and almond meal in the bowl of a stand mixer fitted with
the paddle attachment. Mix together on medium speed until smooth and fluffy, about
1 minute. Add the egg yolks and vanilla and mix until thoroughly combined, scraping
the sides of the bowl often, about 20 seconds. On low speed, add the flour and mix
just until incorporated, about 1 minute. Form the dough into a flattened circle and wrap
it in plastic wrap. Refrigerate for 1 hour, minimum.

GRAPEFRUIT SYRUP

30 g Soaking Syrup (page 198)

10 g pink grapefruit juice

In a small bowl, combine the syrup with the juice. Set aside.

LAVENDER CRÈME BRÛLÉE

150 g heavy cream

1 g (1.5 tsp) culinary-grade dried lavender

45 g egg yolks

35 g sugar

Preheat the oven to 300°F (150°C). Place a 15-cavity 4-centimeter (1.5-in) silicone dome mold on a half sheet pan.

In a small saucepan, bring the cream to a boil. Remove it from the heat and add the lavender. Cover and infuse for 15 minutes. Strain the cream and discard the lavender.

Place the cream, egg yolks and sugar in a small bowl and blend them with an immersion blender. Fill the mold with the crème brûlée. Pass the flame of a propane torch over the surface of the cavities to pop any bubbles. Place the pan in the oven, but before closing the door pour 1 centimeter (0.5 in) of warm tap water into the pan around the mold for more even cooking. Close the door and bake until the crème brûlée is set, 25 to 30 minutes. When you lightly shake the pan, the crème brûlée should not move in the center. Allow to cool to room temperature, pour the water out of the pan and then place it in the freezer. Freeze for at least 4 hours.

Before baking, pass a torch over the crème brûlée to pop any bubbles.

The crème brûlée is done when it no longer moves.

Remove the water in the pan before freezing.

ALMOND CREAM

65 g unsalted butter

65 g sugar

5 g (1 tsp) vanilla extract

50 g eggs

65 g almond meal

14 g pastry flour

Place the butter and sugar in the bowl of the stand mixer fitted with the paddle attachment. Mix on high speed until incorporated and lighter in texture, about 2 minutes. In a small bowl, mix the vanilla with the eggs. Add half of the eggs to the butter mixture and continue to mix, scraping down the sides of the bowl as needed, until combined. Add the rest of the eggs and repeat. Add the almond meal and the flour. Mix on low speed just until combined, about 15 seconds.

GRAPEFRUIT MOUSSE

2 g (scant ½ tsp) powdered gelatin

10 g cold water

125 g milk

3 g pink grapefruit zest (from about 1 grapefruit)

25 g egg yolks

32 g sugar

10 g cornstarch

12 g unsalted butter

40 g pink grapefruit juice

50 g heavy cream

1 drop red food coloring (optional)

Place a 15-cavity 4-centimeter (1.5-in) silicone dome mold on a half sheet pan.

In a small bowl, combine the gelatin with the cold water and stir well to dissolve. Let sit for 5 minutes to bloom.

In a small saucepan, bring the milk to a boil. Remove from the heat and add the zest. Cover and infuse for 15 minutes. Strain the milk and discard the zest.

In a medium bowl, combine the egg yolks, sugar and cornstarch and immediately whisk until the mixture turns pale, about 10 seconds. Slowly whisk the milk into the egg mixture and then strain it into a clean saucepan.

Over medium heat, whisk continually until the mixture starts to thicken, about 1 to 2 minutes. Pull off the heat and keep whisking while the mixture continues to thicken from the residual heat. Return to the heat, still whisking, until the mixture boils, being careful not to burn the bottom. Remove from the heat, add the butter and stir until it melts. Stir in the grapefruit juice. Next, add the gelatin mixture to the warm pastry cream and stir to melt. Pour into a medium bowl and allow to cool to 90°F (32°C).

In a medium bowl, whisk the heavy cream by hand to stiff peak. When the pastry cream is at the correct temperature, fold half of the heavy cream into the pastry cream, using a whisk, followed by the second half. Add the food coloring, if desired. Fill the cavities of the mold with the mousse and level off with a small offset spatula. Freeze for at least 4 hours.

ASSEMBLY

15 g pistachios, chopped

1 pink grapefruit, sectioned

Fresh lavender, as desired

Preheat the oven to 350°F (175°C). Roll out the almond tart dough to a thickness of 0.5 centimeters (0.2 in). Line a 20-centimeter (8-in) tart shell or ring with the dough and chill for at least 20 minutes. Before baking, weigh the dough down with flour wrapped in plastic wrap (see Techniques, page 195).

Bake until the edges look set, about 15 minutes. Remove the plastic and continue to bake until the bottom of the tart is dry to the touch and barely starting to brown, about 10 minutes. Add the almond cream in spoonfuls over the bottom of the tart. Return it to the oven for 2 minutes to allow the cream to partially melt. Remove the tart from the oven and spread the cream to cover the entire bottom. Return it to the oven and bake until the almond cream is set, 16 to 18 minutes. Brush the almond cream with the grapefruit syrup. Allow to cool.

Unmold the frozen crème brûlée and mousse domes. Place them interchangeably on the almond cream to cover the surface. Fill the voids in between the domes with chopped pistachios so you cannot see any almond cream. Cut the grapefruit sections in half and place them between the domes closest to the tart shell edge. Add fresh lavender between the domes for décor.

THE CHA-CHA

DIFFICULTY:

Let's dance.

Cha-cha cherries, cha-cha chocolate . . . throw in some amaretto and we've got a party.
Don't forget the crunchy, salted almonds; sweet caramelized crème brûlée top and a
touch of gold leaf to make your eyes sparkle.

For this recipe, you will need a 20-centimeter (8-in) tart ring and a 15-centimeter (6-in)
disk-shaped silicone mold for the amaretto crème brûlée.

YIELD: 10 servings

ALMOND TART DOUGH

100 g unsalted butter, at room
temperature

50 g powdered sugar

1 g (⅛ tsp) salt

40 g almond meal

60 g egg yolks

2.5 g (½ tsp) vanilla extract

165 g all-purpose flour

Place the butter, sugar, salt and almond meal in the bowl of a stand mixer fitted with
the paddle attachment. Mix together on medium speed until smooth and fluffy, about
1 minute. Add the egg yolks and vanilla and mix until thoroughly combined, scraping
the sides of the bowl often, about 20 seconds. On low speed, add the flour and mix
just until incorporated, about 1 minute. Form the dough into a flattened circle and wrap
it in plastic wrap. Refrigerate for 1 hour, minimum.

AMARETTO CRÈME BRÛLÉE

40 g milk

100 g heavy cream

40 g egg yolks

25 g sugar, plus more for sprinkling

20 g amaretto

1 g (¼ tsp) vanilla extract

Preheat the oven to 300°F (150°C). Place a 15-centimeter (6-in) disk-shaped silicone mold on a half sheet pan.

Place all the crème brûlée ingredients in a small bowl and blend them with an immersion blender. Fill the mold with the crème brûlée. Pass the flame of a propane torch over the surface of the cavities to pop any bubbles. Place the pan in the oven, but before closing the door, pour 1 centimeter (0.5 in) of warm tap water into the pan around the mold for more even cooking. Close the door and bake until the crème brûlée is set, for about 30 to 40 minutes. When you lightly shake the pan, the crème brûlée should not move in the center. Allow to cool to room temperature, pour the water out of the pan and then place it in the freezer. Freeze for at least 4 hours.

ALMOND CREAM

65 g unsalted butter

65 g sugar

5 g (1 tsp) vanilla extract

50 g eggs

65 g almond meal

14 g pastry flour

Place the butter and sugar in the bowl of the stand mixer fitted with the paddle attachment. Mix on high speed until incorporated and lighter in texture, about 2 minutes. In a small bowl, mix the vanilla with the eggs. Add half of the eggs to the bowl and continue to mix, scraping down the sides of the bowl as needed, until combined. Add the rest of the eggs and repeat. Add the almond meal and the flour. Mix on low speed just until combined, about 15 seconds.

CHOCOLATE CREAM

85 g dark chocolate

100 g milk

100 g heavy cream

40 g egg yolks

20 g sugar

Place the chocolate in a bowl with a strainer over it.

In a small saucepan, combine the milk, cream, egg yolks and sugar and blend with an immersion blender. Over low heat, stir the mixture constantly with a heat-safe rubber spatula. When it reaches 180°F (82°C) immediately strain it over the chocolate. Let sit for 1 minute to allow the chocolate to melt and then blend with an immersion blender until smooth. Use immediately (see Assembly).

ASSEMBLY

60 g brandied cherries

25 g almonds, roasted and salted (use Spanish Marcona almonds, if possible)

14 fresh cherries (remove stems from all but 2)

Gold leaf, as desired

Preheat the oven to 350°F (175°C).

Roll the tart dough to a thickness of 0.5 centimeter (0.2 in). Line a 20-centimeter (8-in) tart shell or ring with the dough and chill for at least 20 minutes. Before baking, weigh the dough down with flour wrapped in plastic wrap (see Techniques, page 195).

Bake until the edges look set, about 15 minutes. Remove the plastic and continue to bake until the bottom of the tart is dry to the touch and barely starting to brown, about 10 minutes. Add the almond cream in spoonfuls over the bottom of the tart. Return it to the oven for 2 minutes to allow the cream to partially melt. Remove the tart from the oven and spread the cream to cover the entire bottom. Evenly stud the cream with the brandied cherries and almonds. Return it to the oven and bake until the almond cream is set, 16 to 18 minutes. The almond cream may seem a bit wet around the cherries, but it will dry out as it cools.

Prepare the chocolate cream. Pour the chocolate cream over the almond cream to cover completely. Unmold the frozen amaretto crème brûlée disk and place it in the center of the tart, pushing gently so the edges are barely submerged in the chocolate cream.

Sprinkle the crème brûlée with a thin even layer of sugar. Caramelize the sugar with a propane torch, using the lowest setting, being careful not to heat the sugar too much in one spot or it may burn.

Arrange the stemless fresh cherries around the crème brûlée. Place the 2 cherries with stems on the crème brûlée and top them with gold leaf.

CHAPTER THREE

COUPES

The parfait's more sophisticated sibling. Coupes are desserts consisting of multiple recipes and layered in a glass. An easy way to create individual-sized desserts and to show off that vintage glassware you forgot you had. Whether you're using an antique beer stein for the Beer Float (page 97) or a mason jar to easily transport your house-made "Nutella" in I Pity the Fool (page 73), have fun with these recipes and show them off in the vessel of your choice. No special molds or equipment needed here (well, maybe a record player), and since these recipes don't need to be unmolded, we can also eliminate the use of gelatin for the most part.

I PITY THE FOOL

DIFFICULTY:

. . . who actually eats that ubiquitous processed hazelnut spread with more
ingredients than necessary.

Bring your A-game to the table and make it from scratch. Skip the palm oil and use quality
chocolate and fresh cream and hazelnut paste. The rich ganache is balanced by a light, airy crème
légère, and the chocolate pearls are added for a nice crunch and fun presentation. By serving
these in jars with lids, they are perfect for transport when you are called on to bring dessert.
Like little presents for every guest!

YIELD: 10 jars

HAZELNUT GANACHE

65 g milk chocolate

165 g dark chocolate

Pinch of salt

400 g heavy cream

50 g glucose syrup or corn syrup

230 g sugar

60 g unsweetened hazelnut paste

Place the chocolates and salt in a medium bowl with a strainer over it and set aside. In a small saucepan, bring the cream to a simmer. Remove it from the heat and set aside.

In a large saucepan, melt the glucose over medium heat, about 30 seconds. Add half of the sugar and stir. Allow the sugar to melt a bit, about 30 seconds, and stir again. Add the rest of the sugar and stir. Allow to melt a bit and stir again. Continue to cook, stirring, until the sugar is a deep golden caramel color, about 2 minutes. Remove from the heat and immediately add the hot cream, one-third at a time, stirring after each addition. The hot caramel will foam up. Let the foam subside before the next addition. After all the cream is added, strain the caramel over the bowl of chocolate.

Let the mixture sit for 1 minute to melt the chocolate, then blend it smooth with an immersion blender. Add the hazelnut paste and continue to mix until smooth. While warm, pour the ganache into 10 (235-milliliter [8-oz]) canning jars, 75 grams per jar. Refrigerate.

CRÈME LÉGÈRE

500 g milk

100 g egg yolks

125 g sugar

40 g cornstarch

25 g unsalted butter, softened

250 g heavy cream

5 g (1 tsp) vanilla extract

Prepare a pastry cream: place the milk, yolks, sugar, cornstarch and butter in a microwave-safe medium bowl. Blend them with an immersion blender and then place the bowl in the microwave. Cook on high until the top and sides of the pastry cream are set and jiggle like Jell-O when you shake the bowl, 5 to 7 minutes. The center will still be a bit liquid and the sides almost curdled. With a clean immersion blender, mix the pastry cream to combine, scrape the sides of the bowl and continue to blend in the center and also just at the surface until smooth. If, after blending, the cream is still very runny and has not thickened, continue to cook and blend until you have the consistency of pudding. Cover the surface with plastic wrap and refrigerate immediately.

In a medium bowl, combine the cream with vanilla and whisk to stiff peak.

Transfer the cooled pastry cream to the bowl of a stand mixer fitted with the paddle attachment. Mix on medium-high speed until smooth, about 30 seconds. Fold the whipped cream into the pastry cream.

ASSEMBLY

100 g dark chocolate pearls (I recommend the Crunchy Pearls by Valrhona or the Crispy Pearls by Callebaut)

Gold leaf, as desired

Pipe 90 grams of crème légère into each jar on top of the cooled hazelnut ganache. Top with the chocolate pearls and a touch of gold leaf.

FROU-FROU

DIFFICULTY:

Fancy treats for fancy people.

This is a light, airy cream that just gets brighter with the addition of fresh fruit.
Feel free to swap out the kiwi and strawberries with whatever is in season.
The final toasting of the top is the crème de la crème.

YIELD: 8 servings

WHITE CHOCOLATE CREAM

135 g egg whites

255 g sugar, divided, plus more for sprinkling

68 g water

375 g milk

½ vanilla bean

45 g egg yolks

38 g cornstarch

115 g white chocolate

Prepare an Italian meringue (see page 192) with the egg whites, 225 grams of the sugar and the water. Whisk to cool, about 10 minutes.

Cut the vanilla bean in half again lengthwise. Scrape out the seeds and add them and the pod to a saucepan along with the milk. Bring the milk to a boil, then turn off the heat, cover and infuse for 15 minutes. Strain the milk and discard the vanilla bean.

In a medium bowl, combine the egg yolks, remaining 30 grams of the sugar and half of the cornstarch and immediately whisk until the mixture turns pale, about 10 seconds. Add the rest of the cornstarch and whisk just to combine. Slowly whisk the milk into the egg mixture and then strain it into a clean saucepan.

Over medium heat, whisk continually until the mixture starts to thicken, about 1 to 2 minutes. Pull off the heat and keep whisking while the mixture continues to thicken from the residual heat. Return to the heat, still whisking, until the mixture boils, being careful not to burn the bottom. Remove from the heat and add the chocolate. Stir just until the chocolate is melted, then pour into a large bowl. Allow to cool to room temperature, stirring often.

Stir one-fourth of the meringue into the cream, using a whisk. Add half of the remaining meringue and fold with a spatula until combined. Fold in the rest of the meringue.

ASSEMBLY

16 strawberries

5 kiwi fruit

Sugar, as needed

Hull 8 strawberries and cut them into triangular slices. Arrange the slices around the sides of 8 cocktail glasses. Pipe 35 grams of cream into each glass. Peel and chop 3 of the kiwi and add about 25 grams to each glass. Pipe 55 grams of cream on top of the kiwi.

Sprinkle the tops of the cream with an even, thin layer of sugar. Toast the sugar with a propane torch, using the lowest setting. The tops will resemble toasted marshmallow rather than crème brûlée. Chill the glasses for 20 minutes. Decorate the tops with the remaining kiwi and strawberries.

To make the kiwi décor, slice a small segment off the side. Score the kiwi just down to the skin in a grid pattern.

Push on the skin to invert the kiwi segment.

SPANISH COFFEE

DIFFICULTY: 🍪

411 SW 3rd Ave., Portland

Huber's—home to the Spanish Coffee since 1879. Heavy on the rum. Even heavier on the flair when they light it on fire at your table. We've gathered up some of the same flavors and made a dessert out of them. Ignite at your own risk.

YIELD: 12 servings

PAIN D'ÉPICES

150 g all-purpose flour

2 g (1 tsp) ground cinnamon

0.25 g (⅛ tsp) ground ginger

0.25 g (⅛ tsp) ground cloves

0.75 g (¼ tsp) ground nutmeg

1.5 g (¼ tsp) salt

6 g baking powder

42 g unsalted butter

65 g sugar

100 g honey

60 g eggs

75 g unsweetened yogurt

32 g brewed coffee, at room temperature

Preheat the oven to 350°F (175°C). Line a half sheet pan with a silicone baking mat.

Sift together the flour, spices, salt and baking powder. Set aside.

Place the butter and the sugar in the bowl of a stand mixer fitted with the paddle attachment. Mix on medium speed until well combined, about 4 minutes. Add the honey and mix until combined, about 20 seconds. Add the eggs in two parts, scraping down the bowl as needed as you mix. Add the yogurt and coffee and mix on low speed, about 20 seconds. Add the flour mixture and mix just until combined, about 20 seconds.

Since this is a small quantity, spread the batter on only *half* of the half sheet pan using an offset spatula. Bake until the top is firm to touch and not sticky, about 16 to 18 minutes. Allow to cool completely.

RUM SYRUP

275 g Soaking Syrup (page 198)

90 g dark rum

In a small bowl, combine the syrup with the rum. Set aside.

COFFEE CREAM

30 g coffee beans

450 g milk

160 g egg yolks

110 g sugar

385 g heavy cream

Lightly crush the coffee beans in a plastic bag, using a rolling pin. In a small saucepan, bring the milk to a boil, remove it from heat and add the coffee beans. Cover and infuse for 15 minutes. Strain and discard the beans.

In a small bowl, whisk together the egg yolks and sugar until pale, about 30 seconds. Slowly add the milk while whisking. Transfer the mixture to a medium saucepan with a thermometer. Place a strainer over a clean bowl, next to the stove. Cook the mixture over low heat, stirring constantly with a heat-safe rubber spatula or wooden spoon. When the mixture reaches 180°F (82°C), immediately strain it into the bowl. Refrigerate.

In the bowl of the stand mixer fitted with the whisk attachment, whisk the cream to stiff peak. Remove one-fourth of the whipped cream and whisk it quickly into the coffee mixture. Then pour the coffee mixture into the whipped cream and fold with the whisk until combined.

CINNAMON STREUSEL

40 g unsalted butter

32 g brown sugar

32 g almond meal

40 g pastry flour

Pinch of salt

0.75 g (¼ tsp) ground cinnamon

Preheat the oven to 350°F (175°C). Line a half sheet pan with a silicone baking mat.

Mix the butter with the brown sugar in the bowl of the stand mixer fitted with the paddle attachment until well combined, about 2 minutes.

In a small bowl, stir together the almond meal, flour, salt and cinnamon and then add them to the butter mixture. Mix on low speed until the dough starts clumping together, about 1 minute. Remove the dough from the bowl and form into a single mass.

Break off random shaped pieces about the size of a hazelnut and place them on the pan in a single layer. Bake until lightly golden brown, about 12 to 14 minutes.

ORANGE WHIPPED CREAM

68 g powdered sugar

465 g heavy cream

72 g Grand Marnier

Sift the powdered sugar into the bowl of a stand mixer fitted with the whisk attachment. Add the cream and Grand Marnier and whisk to stiff peak.

ASSEMBLY

35 g pain d'épices

30 g rum syrup

75 g coffee cream

10 g cinnamon streusel

5 g candied orange

Dark alkalized cocoa powder, for décor

75 g candied orange, for décor

Cut the cake into 2-centimeter (0.8-in) squares. Heat the rum syrup until hot.

In a 225-gram (8-oz) Spanish coffee mug, layer the ingredients in order, starting at the bottom of the glass.

Pipe the orange whipped cream on top. Sprinkle with cocoa powder and a few pieces of candied orange.

CHOCOLATE & CHURROS, FRENCHIE STYLE!

DIFFICULTY:

Hola or bonjour?

Chocolate con churros is a popular late-night snack in Madrid. Who doesn't like fried dough after a night on the town and a few glasses of wine? Many churro recipes are dense and don't taste like much more than, well, fried dough. And the drinking chocolate usually contains cornstarch to thicken it, which leaves a skin on the surface if it sits for a minute. Maybe that's why you eat them at four a.m. after copious glasses of wine? Maybe. But let's just make them better, using eggs, butter and cream as the French would do.

YIELD: 10 servings

CHURROS

285 g milk

4 g salt

8 g sugar

130 g unsalted butter

170 g pastry flour

10 g (2 tsp) vanilla extract

160 g eggs

In a medium saucepan, combine the milk, salt, sugar and butter. Warm the mixture over medium heat, stirring occasionally, until the butter is melted, about 3 minutes. Then, bring the mixture to a boil. Remove the pan from the heat, add all the flour at once and stir with a wooden spoon. Return the pan to the stove and continue to heat, stirring, until all the liquid is absorbed and the mixture comes together. Once you see a film of dough on the bottom of the pan and the mixture starts to pull away from the sides and roll toward the middle, about 10 seconds, remove it from the heat. Transfer the mixture to the bowl of a stand mixer fitted with the paddle attachment.

Lightly mix the vanilla and the eggs to break up the yolks. Add a third of the eggs and mix on medium speed until they are completely absorbed, about 30 seconds. Add another third and allow to incorporate. Add the remaining eggs and mix until just combined.

Line a half sheet pan with a piece of parchment. Place the dough in a piping bag fitted with a 2 centimeter (0.8 in) open star tip. Pipe the dough into individual 10-centimeter (4-in) long pieces onto the parchment and freeze for 20 minutes. Partially freezing the dough will help it hold shape when frying. If you want to freeze the churros completely to fry at a later time, allow them to partially defrost before frying. You want the churros still solid enough to handle but not so cold as to drastically lower the temperature of the cooking oil when they are used.

CHOCOLAT CHAUD

60 g egg yolks

350 g milk

150 g heavy cream

300 g dark chocolate

80 g green chartreuse, optional

Place the egg yolks in a medium bowl. In a medium saucepan, bring the milk and cream to a simmer. Remove the mixture from the heat and whisk it slowly into the egg yolks. The heat of the liquid will cook the eggs yolks. Add the chocolate and wait 1 minute. Blend with an immersion blender until smooth.

Now, if you want to really Frenchify this recipe, add 80 grams of green chartreuse. Chartreuse is an herbal liqueur made by monks in the south of France from a secret recipe of over 100 plants and herbs . . . and happens to go great with dark chocolate. Absinthe could also be used.

> PARLOR TRICK! Egg yolks are natural emulsifiers. Adding egg yolks to the chocolat chaud will make it easier to reheat without it separating.

SPICE MIXTURE

200 g sugar

5 g (1 tsp) ground cinnamon

2.5 g (½ tsp) ground cardamom

5 g (1 tsp) ground nutmeg

In a shallow bowl, mix together the sugar and spices.

ASSEMBLY

2000 g canola oil

In a deep pot, heat the canola oil to 350°F (175°C). Add the churros, 4 at a time. After a couple of minutes, the churros will rise to the top of the oil. Use a wire-mesh strainer to try to hold them down. Fry the churros until golden brown, about 4 to 6 minutes. Remove the churros from the oil and place them on a paper towel–lined plate. Roll the churros in the spice mixture.

Pour the warm chocolat chaud into espresso cups (about 75 grams per cup). If it needs reheating, do so in the microwave on a very low heat setting, stirring about every 10 seconds, so it does not burn. Serve with the churros for dunking.

GET THE DOOR. PEDRO'S HERE.

DIFFICULTY:

And he's got the goods.

Pedro Ximénez, often simply referred to as PX, is a sweet style of sherry. It's dark, raisiny and concentrated with a viscosity and sweetness that will knock your socks off. It can be enjoyed as a dessert in itself, but is often poured over vanilla ice cream like a sauce. I like to pair PX with blue cheese. The saltiness of the cheese plays wonderfully with the sweetness of the wine. That being said, the ultimate pairing? PX and blue cheese ice cream! Any blue cheese will work for this recipe. Choose one whose intensity and saltiness suits your palate. And visit your local wine shop for a quality PX sherry. Once opened, the sherry will stay fresh for weeks.

YIELD: 12 servings

BLUE CHEESE ICE CREAM

1 vanilla bean

450 g milk

150 g heavy cream

120 g egg yolks

150 g sugar

70 g blue cheese

100 g dark chocolate

15 g cocoa nibs

Cut the vanilla bean in half lengthwise. Scrape out the seeds and add them and the pod to a medium saucepan along with the milk and cream. Bring to a boil, then turn off the heat, cover and infuse for 15 minutes. Strain the milk and discard the vanilla bean.

In a small bowl, whisk together the egg yolks and sugar until pale, about 10 seconds. Slowly add the milk mixture while whisking. Transfer the mixture to a medium saucepan with a thermometer. Place a strainer over a clean bowl, next to the stove. Cook the mixture over low heat, stirring constantly with a heat-safe rubber spatula. When the mixture reaches 180°F (82°C), immediately strain it into the bowl. Add the blue cheese and blend with an immersion blender. Refrigerate for at least 4 hours to let the flavors mature.

Churn the mixture in an ice-cream maker. After churning, place the ice cream in a wide bowl and put it in the freezer to chill for 10 minutes. Melt the chocolate and stir in the cocoa nibs. Remove the ice cream from the freezer. Drizzle the chocolate into the ice cream while folding. Return the ice cream to the freezer to harden.

ASSEMBLY

One 750 ml bottle Pedro Ximénez sherry, chilled

Place a large scoop of the cream in a champagne coupe or martini glass. Serve 60 grams of Pedro Ximénez in a smaller glass on the side. When ready to eat, pour the Pedro Ximénez over the ice cream and enjoy.

BALLER'S DELIGHT

DIFFICULTY:

Cognac, champagne, Moscato d'Asti. That's where the party's at. If only you were invited!

Ladyfingers have many more uses than just to make tiramisu. They're made for dipping and transporting flavors to your mouth. Those stale cookies packaged in plastic found at the grocery store are no substitute for making your own, which should be consumed the same day. Moscato d'Asti, a lightly sparking, off dry, floral wine, makes a beautifully perfumed, light and fluffy sabayon to dunk your ladyfingers in.

For this recipe, you will need two 5-centimeter (2-in) chocolate demisphere molds to make the disco balls.

YIELD: 8 servings

LADYFINGERS

60 g egg yolks

90 g granulated sugar, divided

5 g (1 tsp) vanilla extract

10 g (2 tsp) water

90 g egg whites

90 g pastry flour

Powdered sugar

Preheat the oven to 375°F (190°C). Place a half sheet pan on the oven floor and fill it a third of the way up with water. Place the egg yolks in the bowl of a stand mixer fitted with the whisk attachment and whisk with 30 grams of the granulated sugar on high speed until thick and pale, about 5 minutes. Transfer the yolk mixture to a larger bowl with a wide surface area on top. Fold in the vanilla and water.

Prepare a French meringue (see page 191) with the egg whites and the remaining 60 grams of granulated sugar, whisking to very stiff peak.

Sift one-fourth of the flour onto the yolk mixture in a thin layer, covering the top. Gently fold in the flour and repeat with another fourth. If you add too much flour at once it could clump up in the batter. Gently fold in half of the meringue. Then, sift the remaining flour onto the batter and fold to combine. Fold in the remaining meringue just until incorporated. Careful not to overmix.

Place the mixture in a piping bag fitted with a 1-centimeter (0.5-in) tip. Pipe the ladyfingers 7.5 centimeters (3 in) long on two sheets of parchment paper. Sift a light layer of powdered sugar over the ladyfingers and let them sit for 5 minutes to absorb the sugar. Sift a more generous second layer of powdered sugar on the ladyfingers and let sit for another 5 minutes.

(continued)

LADYFINGERS (CONTINUED)

Grab the top corners of the parchment and lift them up. Shake gently onto the counter to remove the excess sugar. If your meringue was stiff and your mixing was gentle, the ladyfingers will stay in place. Place the parchment flat on half sheet pans and place a second pan under them. Put the pans in the oven, leaving the pan of water on the floor of the oven. The water will add humidity that will give the ladyfingers the traditional bead look on top as the sugar caramelizes. Bake the ladyfingers just until they start to brown, about 10 to 12 minutes. The finished ladyfingers should be crisp on the outside but soft on the inside. Use the same day or freeze in an airtight container until ready to use.

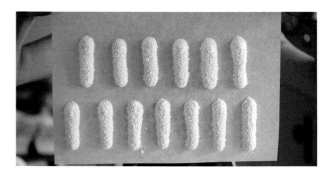

CHOCOLATE DISCO BALLS

800 g dark chocolate

70 g dark chocolate pearls (Crunchy Pearls by Valrhona or Crispy Pearls by Callebaut)

Assorted luster dust color, as needed

Silver cake sparkles, as needed

PARLOR TRICK! By chilling the chocolate and then bringing it back to room temperature, we are encouraging condensation. The damp surface will draw some of the sugars in the chocolate to the surface, making it slightly sticky and allowing the sparkles to adhere.

Temper the chocolate in the microwave (see Techniques, page 190). Pour half the chocolate into the first mold to fill all the cavities. Tap the mold on the edge of the counter fast and vigorously for a few seconds to release any air bubbles. Flip the mold upside down, holding it over a piece of parchment. Tap the side of the mold with a wide metal scraper to get rid of the excess chocolate. Scrape the top of the mold smooth and place it upside down on a clean piece of parchment. After 1 minute, lift up the mold and scrape the top clean with the metal scraper. Place it, right side up, in the refrigerator and chill for 5 minutes, to set the chocolate. Repeat with the second mold. Remove the molds from the refrigerator and let sit for another 10 minutes.

Roll the chocolate pearls in the luster dust colors. Place them in a small strainer and tap it to remove any excess color. Add 8 grams of the chocolate pearls to 8 of the demi mold cavities.

Slide the other 8 pieces out of the second mold. Use a propane torch to heat part of a metal scraper. Place a demisphere briefly on the hot surface just until it starts melting, then attach it to one of the other halves still in the mold. Continue with the rest and place the mold back in the refrigerator to chill for 3 minutes.

Pierce each chocolate ball with a toothpick and place the toothpick into a piece of Styrofoam to hold up the chocolate. Refrigerate the chocolate for 20 minutes. Remove the chocolate from the refrigerator and leave at room temperature for another 5 minutes. Holding the toothpick, cover the chocolate with the cake sparkles and place them back in the Styrofoam until ready to use.

MOSCATO D'ASTI SABAYON

160 g egg yolks

200 g sugar

200 g Moscato d'Asti

Place an inch of water in a small saucepan and bring to a simmer. Place the egg yolks in the bowl of the stand mixer, add the sugar and immediately whisk by hand. Place the bowl over the pot of simmering water and heat, whisking constantly, until the mixture reaches 131°F (55°C). Immediately remove the bowl from the heat and transfer it to the mixer fitted with the whisk attachment. Whisk on high speed until the yolks look very thick and pale, about 5 minutes.

Warm the Moscato d'Asti to 131°F (55°C). While still whisking on high speed, pour the wine very slowly down the inside of the bowl into the yolks. The yolks will loosen up again to a runny consistency. Continue to whisk at high speed until the sabayon is thick and fluffy, about 8 minutes. Use immediately (see Assembly).

ASSEMBLY

400 g cantaloupe

Cut the cantaloupe into spheres, using a very small melon baller.

Place 50 grams of cantaloupe in 8 (340-gram [12-oz]) wine glasses. Top with 60 grams of Moscato d'Asti sabayon. Arrange a couple of ladyfingers on top of the glass to hold the disco ball. Serve within the hour on a hundred-dollar bill for a coaster and more ladyfingers for dipping.

CHAI

DIFFICULTY:

Jazz up your next tea party with this chai dessert. Here the popular spiced tea, masala chai, is tranformed into a dessert that you eat instead of drink. The génoise soaks up the chai cream like a sponge, leaving it moist and flavorful. For a bit of crunch, the tea is topped with a cookie flavored with quatre épices. Quatre épices is an equal blend of four ground spices, usually white pepper, cloves, nutmeg and ginger. You can make any size spice blend you like and then measure out what you need. Make sure you assemble the cups right before serving, so the components don't become soggy.

YIELD: 8 servings

GÉNOISE

170 g eggs

95 g sugar, plus more for dusting

95 g pastry flour

30 g unsalted butter, melted

1.5 g (1 tsp) fine orange zest

Preheat the oven to 350°F (175°C). Line a half sheet pan with a silicone baking mat.

Place 2.5 centimeters (1 in) of water in a small saucepan and bring it to a simmer. Place the eggs in the bowl of a stand mixer. Add the sugar and mix with a hand whisk to combine. Place the bowl over the pot of simmering water and heat, whisking constantly, until the mixture reaches 105°F (40°C). Immediately remove the bowl from the heat and transfer it to the mixer fitted with the whisk attachment. Whisk on high speed until the bottom of the bowl is cool to the touch and the batter is light and fluffy, about 5 minutes. When the whisk is removed, the batter should fall on itself without sinking.

Transfer the batter into a larger bowl with a wide surface area on top and add the orange zest. Sift one-fourth of the flour onto the batter in a thin layer covering the top. Gently fold the flour into the batter and then repeat, one-fourth at a time, until all the flour is incorporated. Pour the melted butter over the top and fold just until combined. Do not overmix. Ideally, if you have a helper in the kitchen, have the person continually sift the flour over the batter while you continually fold. If you add too much flour at once, it could clump up in the batter.

Since this is a small quantity, spread the batter on only half of the half sheet pan. Bake until the top is dry to the touch and golden brown, 18 to 20 minutes.

SPICED COOKIE

80 g unsalted butter, softened

65 g brown sugar

65 g hazelnut meal

25 g pailleté feuilletine

65 g all-purpose flour

1½ g (½ tsp) quatre épices

Preheat the oven to 350°F (175°C).

Place the butter and brown sugar in the bowl of the stand mixer fitted with the paddle attachment. Mix on high speed until well combined and smooth, about 2 minutes. Add the hazelnut meal, pailleté feuilletine, flour and quatre épices and mix on low speed until sandy, about 1 minute.

Pour onto a silicone baking mat and squeeze the mixture in your hands until it starts to stick together. Top it with a second silicone baking mat, smooth side down. Roll the dough between the smooth sides of the mats to a thickness of about 0.5 centimeters (0.2 in). Slide the mats onto a half sheet pan and freeze for 10 minutes so the dough is easier to handle.

Peel off the top mat and replace it with a piece of parchment. Flip the pan over so the parchment is on the counter. Remove the second mat. Cut out 8 circles that are about 1 centimeter (0.5 in) smaller than the top of your teacups. Place the circles on a half sheet pan lined with a silicone baking mat. Bake until golden brown, 10 to 12 minutes.

CHAI CREAM

1100 g milk

10 g fresh ginger, peeled and sliced

14 g fennel seeds

3 g (14) green cardamom pods

3 g (28) whole cloves

10 g (2) cinnamon stick

3 g (62) black peppercorn

20 g black tea (such as Indian Assam)

280 g egg yolks

220 g sugar

In a medium saucepan, bring the milk to a boil. Remove it from the heat and add the spices. Cover and infuse for 10 minutes. Add the tea and continue to infuse for 4 minutes or as directed by the producer. Strain the milk and discard the spices and tea. Bring the milk back to a boil and then remove from the heat.

Place the egg yolks in a medium bowl. Add one-fourth of the sugar to a large saucepan and cook over medium heat. When you see the edges start to melt, about 1 minute, stir briefly with a wooden spoon and allow the edges to melt again. Stir again and repeat until all the sugar is melted. It will have a light, opaque caramel color. Add the rest of the sugar, one-fourth at a time, following the same procedure.

Continue to cook, stirring, until the sugar is a deep golden caramel color, about 2 minutes. Slowly add the hot milk, little by little, batting the rising foam back and forth with your spoon until it subsides. If some of the caramel seizes up after all the milk is added, continue to cook on low heat until it dissolves. Slowly whisk the milk into the egg yolks.

Place the mixture into a clean medium saucepan with a thermometer. Place a strainer over a clean bowl, next to the stove. Cook the mixture over low heat, stirring constantly with a heat-safe rubber spatula. When the mixture reaches 180°F (82°C), immediately strain it into the bowl. Refrigerate. Blend with an immersion blender before using.

ORANGE CRÈME CHANTILLY

25 g powdered sugar

250 g cream

5 g (1 tbsp) orange zest

3 g (½ tsp) gelatin, powdered

15 g water, cold

Sift the powdered sugar into a medium bowl and set aside.

Bring the cream to a boil. Remove it from the heat and add the orange zest. Cover and infuse for 15 minutes. While the zest is infusing, combine the gelatin with the cold water and stir well until combined. Let sit 5 minutes to bloom.

Strain the cream into the bowl with the powdered sugar and discard the zest. Add the gelatin to the warm cream and stir until it is melted. Place a piece of plastic wrap directly on the surface of the cream to cover it completely and prevent a skin from forming as it cools. Refrigerate for at least two hours.

Place the cold cream in a mixing bowl. Whisk the cream until stiff peak, about 4 minutes. It will take the cream a little longer to whisk than usual because we heated it, but it will get there. Use immediately (see Assembly, page 96).

ASSEMBLY

Granulated sugar, for dusting

Orange zest, as needed

Gold leaf, as desired

Lightly dust the top of the génoise with granulated sugar so it will not stick when unmolding. Cut around the edges to break the cake away from the sides of the pan. Place a piece of parchment over the cake and flip it upside down. Peel off the silicone mat slowly, starting at one corner and pulling the mat not up, but almost parallel to the mat itself in the opposite direction.

For each tea cup, cut three 5 centimeter (2 in) circles out of the génoise. Stack the cake circles in a column in the center of the cups. Add enough chai cream to the cup to surround the cake column and almost reach the top.

Place the crème chantilly meringue in a medium piping bag with a piping tip of your choice. Pipe a decorative design on each spice cookie.

Zest an orange with a plane zester 7.5 centimeters (3 in) above the cream. Add a touch of gold leaf and place the cookies on top of the génoise. Serve immediately.

PARLOR TRICK! To achieve the design shown with the crème chantilly, use a record player on a speed of 45 rpms that will turn itself at a constant pace. Place a small inverted dish over the center pin to create a flat surface. Center a spice cookie on top of the dish. Using a rose petal tip, narrow side facing up, slowly move the piping tip in a straight line toward the outer edge with the player spinning.

BEER FLOAT

DIFFICULTY:

The best part is when the ice cream starts melting.

Perfect for the adults at your next ice-cream social—the beer float. Half dessert, half meal on its own. A chocolate stout is the preferred beer for this recipe, but you could also use other stouts, porters or a barleywine. Malted barley can be purchased at a home brewers store or online. The pearl barley found in grocery stores is not the same and therefore not a substitute.

YIELD: 8 servings

COFFEE ICE CREAM

80 g coffee beans

1 vanilla bean

750 g milk

250 g heavy cream

200 g egg yolks

250 g sugar

Lightly crush the coffee beans in a plastic bag, using a rolling pin. Cut the vanilla bean in half lengthwise. Scrape out the seeds and add them and the pod to a saucepan along with the milk and cream. Bring to a boil, then remove from the heat and add the coffee beans. Cover and infuse for 15 minutes, then strain and discard the vanilla and coffee beans.

In a small bowl, whisk together the egg yolks and sugar until pale, about 15 seconds. Slowly add the milk mixture while whisking. Transfer the mixture to a medium saucepan and attach a thermometer. Place a strainer over a clean bowl, next to the stove. Cook the mixture over low heat, stirring constantly with a heat-safe rubber spatula. When the mixture reaches 180°F (82°C), immediately strain it into the bowl. Refrigerate for at least 4 hours to let the flavors mature.

Churn the mixture in an ice-cream maker. After churning, place the ice cream in the freezer to harden.

CARAMELIZED MALTED BARLEY

50 g sugar

12 g water

80 g roasted malted barley

Heavy pinch of salt

200 g dark chocolate

Place a silicone baking mat on a half sheet pan.

In a small saucepan, combine the sugar and water. Heat the sugar until it reaches 240°F (116°C). Add the barley and the salt and stir with a wooden spoon to coat. Continue to cook over medium heat, stirring about every 5 seconds. The sugar will seize up and crystalize. Then, with time, the sugar will melt again and caramelize. As it starts to caramelize, stir constantly. The barley should start popping. Once it is coated in a golden brown caramel, about 2 to 4 minutes, remove it from the heat and pour onto the silicone mat. Spread into a single layer and allow to cool.

Break the caramelized barley into decorative pieces. Temper the chocolate (see Techniques, page 190). Dip one-third of each piece into the chocolate. Tap off any excess chocolate and place the pieces on the rough side of a silicone mat, to set up.

ASSEMBLY

8 (330-ml [11-oz]) bottles chocolate stout beer

8 chocolate curls (see Techniques, page 190)

Place a scoop of ice cream into the bottom of a pint glass. Slowly fill the glass halfway with chocolate stout. When the foam subsides, continue to add beer to fill the mug. Place 2 more scoops of ice cream on the rim of the glass. Garnish with the caramelized malted barley and chocolate curls. Serve any remaining beer in the bottle as a beer back.

CHAPTER FOUR

ENTREMETS

Entremets are desserts that combine several recipes to create something multidimensional, blending different textures and flavors in every bite for a very unique eating experience. These are the show-stoppers, showing off both personality and technique. Have a friend who's a chocolate lover? Sure, you could bake a chocolate cake for his or her birthday. Or you could make the Chocolate Pandemonium (page 111)—chocolate mousse, chocolate ganache, chocolate meringue, all molded into a disk and sprayed with more chocolate from a paint sprayer. This Thanksgiving, say you'll bring the pie, but show up with pumpkin bavarois molded with spiced pecans, salted caramel and chocolate almond cake, suitably named Bye, Bye Pumpkin Pie (page 115). Dessert dash at the daughter's elementary school? School them with your mad cream puff skills—the Confetti (page 107) is part fruit tart, part rainbow of cream puff poppers.

The molded entremets in this chapter have unique designs. But if you have just one 20-centimeter (8-in) cake ring, you can layer the recipes of any of the entremets into a circle. While the entire instructions are longer than typical dessert recipes, most of the components can be made in stages and stored in the freezer. They are definitely worth the effort and you will certainly amaze yourself with what you've accomplished.

THE RICKY RICARDO

DIFFICULTY:

Honey, I'm home!

You may think of honey as simply an ingredient and not necessarily a flavor on its own.
But there are a myriad of honeys available these days. Use your favorite because the honey's
flavor will really show through in this dessert. There's also a nod to the South with
some peaches and pecans.

For this recipe, we used a 15-centimeter (6-in) Silikomart "Magia del Tempo" mold (see Sources)
for the honey mousse. You can use any mold of the same size for the center. You will also need
one 15-centimeter (6-in) cake ring, or disk-shaped silicone mold, and one
20-centimeter (8-in) cake ring.

YIELD: 10 servings

HONEY MOUSSE

275 g heavy cream

8 g powdered gelatin

40 g cold water

135 g honey

70 g egg yolks

Place a 15-centimeter (6-in) silicone mold on a half sheet pan.

In the bowl of a stand mixer fitted with the whisk attachment, whisk the cream to soft peak. In a medium, microwave-safe bowl, combine the gelatin with the cold water and stir well to dissolve. Let sit for 5 minutes to bloom.

In a small saucepan, bring the honey to full boil. Meanwhile, in a separate bowl of the stand mixer, start whisking the egg yolks on medium speed. Slowly pour the hot honey down the side of the bowl into the yolks. Increase the speed to high and whisk for 1 minute. Scrape down the sides of the bowl and continue to whisk on high speed until the bowl is cool to the touch, about 5 minutes.

Melt the gelatin on low in the microwave. Swirl the bowl to stir the gelatin every 30 seconds, until it is completely melted. While whisking constantly by hand, slowly pour one-third of the yolk mixture into the gelatin. Switch to a spatula and quickly fold in the remaining yolks. Add one-third of the cream and quickly stir to combine. Add the remaining cream and fold to combine. Pour into the mold. Freeze overnight.

PEACH COULIS

150 g peach puree

32 g sugar

1 cinnamon stick

3 g (½ tsp) powdered gelatin

15 g cold water

Place a 15-centimeter (6-in) disk-shaped silicone mold on a half sheet pan. Alternatively, you can use a cake ring of the same size. Place the cake ring on a piece of parchment. Pull the parchment up the outer sides of the ring and secure it with a large rubber band.

In a small saucepan, combine the puree, sugar and cinnamon stick and bring it to a simmer. Remove from the heat, cover and infuse for 15 minutes.

In a small bowl, combine the gelatin with the cold water and stir well to dissolve. Let sit for 5 minutes to bloom.

Discard the cinnamon stick. Add the solid gelatin mass to the puree and stir until the gelatin is melted. Pour into the mold. Freeze for at least 4 hours.

PECAN BASE

Pan release spray

80 g pecans

20 g all-purpose flour, plus more for dusting

100 g egg whites

100 g powdered sugar

100 g granulated sugar

Preheat the oven to 350°F (175°C). Place a 20-centimeter (8-in) cake ring and on a half sheet lined with a silicone baking mat. Cut a piece of parchment lengthwise into 2 (7.5 cm [3 in])-long strips. Spray them with pan release, dust with flour and then line them around the inside of the cake ring, flour side facing inside.

Grind the pecans in a food processor just until you have small pieces, about 10 seconds. Add the powdered sugar and flour and process to a fine powder, about 20 seconds more. Transfer the mixture to a large bowl.

Prepare a French meringue (see page 191) with the egg whites and granulated sugar, whisking to stiff peak. Due to the high proportion of sugar to egg whites in this recipe, you can whisk away with confidence, as there is little risk of overwhisking the meringue. Add the meringue to the pecan mixture. Gently fold the two together. The mixture should be light and fluffy, not runny, when finished.

Place the batter in a piping bag fitted with a 1-centimeter (0.5-in) open piping tip. Starting in the center of the circle, pipe a spiral toward the cake ring to cover the bottom completely. Pipe 2.5-centimeter (1-in) balls all around the inside edge to create a border. Bake until just lightly golden, about 25 minutes. The base should be crisp on the outside but chewy on the inside.

WHITE CHOCOLATE GLAZE

8 g powdered gelatin

40 g cold water

75 g water

150 g sugar

150 g glucose syrup or corn syrup

100 g sweetened condensed milk

150 g white chocolate

Orange food coloring, as desired

Yellow food coloring, as desired

In a small bowl, combine the gelatin with the cold water and stir well to dissolve. Let sit for 5 minutes to bloom.

In a small saucepan over medium-high heat, cook the remaining 75 grams of water, sugar and glucose to 217°F (103°C). Remove from the heat and pour into a small bowl along with the condensed milk. Add the gelatin mixture and the chocolate and let sit for 1 minute, then mix with an immersion blender until smooth. Blend in the food coloring until the desired shade is reached. Set aside at room temperature.

ASSEMBLY

Powdered sugar, as needed

3 fresh peaches

Gold leaf, as desired

This peach décor is easiest to cut with firmer fruit.

Unmold the base and remove the parchment paper. Dust the outer edge with powdered sugar and then place it on a cake board or platter.

Unmold the coulis and place it in the center of the base. If it does not sit flat in the center, trim the edges until it fits.

In a medium saucepan, warm the glaze to 93°F (34°C). Place the dessert on a wire rack over a half sheet pan. With the glaze at the correct temperature, quickly and generously pour it over the mousse, making sure all the sides are covered. Let it sit for 1 minute. Using a large offset spatula, lift up the mousse slightly. Move it in small circular motions against the rack to remove any excess glaze from the bottom. Place it on top of the coulis.

Cut small segments from the peaches while still on the pit. Tuck them end over end around the mousse. Cut 3 larger peach wedges. Lay each one on its side and cut out a smaller wedge, followed by an even smaller wedge. Reassemble the wedges and feather the pieces upward. Arrange them in a decorative pattern in the center of the mousse and add a touch of gold leaf.

RABELO

DIFFICULTY:

Sailing down the Douro, bringing you the port.

Light, creamy port mousse matches perfectly with the spiced cake and figs in this entremet, while the almonds give a contrast in texture as well as a hint of salt. The flavors meld together like a mulled wine. I recommend using a high-quality tawny port, such as Taylor Fladgate 10 Year. Tawny ports spend time in a barrel before bottling, whereas ruby ports do not. Therefore, a tawny will show flavors of nuts and dried fruit, whereas a ruby port shows flavors of fresh berries, such as blackberries and cherries. For this recipe, you will want to be sure to use a tawny port.

For this recipe, you will need twelve 6.5-centimeter (2.5-in) cake rings or polycarbonate molds and acetate. Alternatively, you could build the ingredients in a 20-centimeter (8-in) cake ring.

YIELD: 12 servings

PORT-SOAKED FIGS

90 g Black Mission figs

125 g tawny port

14 g sugar

1 cinnamon stick

1 star anise, whole

Pull the stems off the figs and cut in half vertically. Place in a small saucepan with the rest of the ingredients and stir to combine. Bring to a simmer and cook over low heat for 10 minutes. Cover with plastic wrap and allow to cool. Remove the spices and puree the mixture in a food processor for 1 minute.

PAIN D'ÉPICES

150 g all-purpose flour

2 g (1 tsp) ground cinnamon

0.25 g (⅛ tsp) ground ginger

0.25 g (⅛ tsp) ground cloves

0.75 g (¼ tsp) ground nutmeg

1.5 g (¼ tsp) salt

6 g baking powder

42 g unsalted butter

65 g sugar

100 g honey

60 g eggs

75 g unsweetened yogurt

32 g brewed coffee, at room temperature

Preheat the oven to 350°F (175°C). Line a half sheet pan with a silicone baking mat.

In a bowl, sift together the flour, spices, salt and baking powder. Set aside.

Place the butter and the sugar in the bowl of a stand mixer fitted with the paddle attachment. Mix on medium speed until well combined, about 4 minutes. Add the honey and mix until combined, about 20 seconds. Add the eggs in two parts, scraping down the bowl as needed as you mix. Add the yogurt and coffee and finish mixing on low speed, about 20 seconds. Add the flour mixture and mix just until combined, about 20 seconds.

Since this is a small quantity, only spread the batter on *half* of the half sheet pan, using an offset spatula. Bake until the top is firm to touch and not sticky, 16 to 18 minutes. Allow to cool completely.

TAWNY PORT MOUSSE

390 g heavy cream

185 g tawny port

110 g sugar

12 g fresh lemon juice

75 g egg yolks

12 g powdered gelatin

60 g cold water

This mousse sets up very quickly. It is important you have all your ingredients and equipment ready before starting to mix it together! (See Assembly, page 109.)

In the bowl of a stand mixer fitted with the whisk attachment, whisk the cream to soft peak and set aside at room temperature.

In a small saucepan, combine the port, sugar and lemon juice and warm it over medium heat to dissolve the sugar, about 2 minutes. Place the egg yolks in a medium bowl. Slowly whisk the warm port mixture into the eggs. Return the mixture to the saucepan.

Rest a strainer on top of the bowl of a stand mixer. Reheat the port mixture over medium heat, stirring constantly with a rubber spatula so the mixture does not stick to the pan. At 180°F (82°C) immediately strain into the prepared bowl. Transfer the bowl to the mixer and whisk the mixture on high speed until the bottom of the bowl is no longer warm to the touch and the mixture is light and airy, about 8 minutes.

While the mixture is cooling, in a medium, microwave-safe bowl, combine the gelatin with the cold water and stir well to dissolve. Let sit for 5 minutes to bloom.

Melt the gelatin on low in the microwave. Swirl the bowl to stir the gelatin every 30 seconds, until it is completely melted. Slowly pour one-third of the port mixture into the gelatin while whisking quickly by hand. Continue to add the rest of the port mixture, now stirring quickly with the whisk. Add half of the cream and stir quickly with the whisk, followed by the second half. Use immediately.

WHITE CHOCOLATE GLAZE

16 g powdered gelatin

80 g cold water

150 g water

300 g sugar

300 g glucose syrup or corn syrup

200 g sweetened condensed milk

300 g white chocolate

Purple food coloring, as desired

In a small bowl, combine the gelatin with the cold water and stir well to dissolve. Let sit for 5 minutes to bloom.

In a small saucepan over medium-high heat, cook the remaining 150 grams of water, the sugar and the glucose to 217°F (103°C). Remove from the heat and pour into a small bowl along with the condensed milk. Add the gelatin and the chocolate and let sit for 1 minute, then mix with an immersion blender until smooth. Reserve 50 grams to use as a white glaze. Blend the food coloring in the remaining glaze until the desired shade is reached. Set aside at room temperature.

ASSEMBLY

Sugar, for dusting

36 g roasted and salted Marcona almond, chopped coarsely

Edible purple and blue flowers

Don't forget to line your molds with acetate or all your work will have been in vain, as you won't be able to get them out!

Line a flat half sheet pan with parchment. Place 12 (6.5 ccentimeter [2.5 in]) individual molds on the pan and line the molds with acetate. Lightly dust the pain d'épices cake top with granulated sugar so it will not stick when unmolding. Cut around the edges to break the cake away from the sides of the pan. Place a piece of parchment over the cake and flip it upside down. Peel the silicone mat off slowly, starting at one corner and pulling the mat not up, but almost parallel to the mat itself in the opposite direction. Cut 12 circles, 5 centimeters (2 in) in diameter, from the pain d'épices and place them onto a half sheet pan lined with parchment. Top each cake circle with 10 grams of the fig mixture and then 3 grams of almonds. Freeze the cakes for at least 30 minutes.

Prepare the mousse. Pipe the molds three-quarters full of mousse, then sink a disk of cake topped with fig puree upside down into the mouse just so the mousse comes up over the sides and the cake is fully in the mold. Top off with more mousse as needed and smooth with an offset spatula. Freeze overnight.

Heat the purple and white chocolate glazes to 93°F (34°C), stirring gently as to not introduce any air bubbles. Unmold the mousse cakes and remove the acetate. Place the cakes on a wire cooling rack with a sheet pan underneath. Pour the purple glaze generously over each cake, adding a few drops of white glaze randomly on top. Quickly use a small offset spatula to push off the excess glaze and smear the white glaze. Lift the mousse cakes off the rack with the offset spatula, first rubbing the bottom of the cakes in a circular motion to discard any excess glaze. Place on a cake board or plate. Decorate with purple and blue flowers.

CONFETTI

The only thing not fun about confetti is cleaning it up.

Half edible rainbow of cream puffs, half deconstructed fruit tart. You can attempt to cut this into pieces but it's more fun to eat the top by just popping the cream puffs in your mouth. The colored craquelin gives the puffs a nice crunch in contrast to the creamy mint crème légère. Be sure to eat this entremet within four hours of filling the puffs and assembling so the pâte à choux stays firm.

YIELD: 12 servings

SWEET TART DOUGH

50 g egg yolks

2.5 g (½ tsp) vanilla extract

155 g all-purpose flour, plus more for rolling and baking

Pinch of salt

70 g powdered sugar

120 g unsalted butter, cold

In a small bowl, whisk together the egg yolks and vanilla and set aside. Sift the flour, salt and sugar into the bowl of a stand mixer fitted with the paddle attachment and combine on low speed. Cut the butter into 1-centimeter (0.5-in) cubes and add it to the bowl. Continue to mix on low until the mixture resembles coarse sand, about 5 minutes. Do not overmix. If the mixture starts to stick together, it will not absorb the eggs and it will be very sticky and hard to roll. Add the egg yolk mixture and mix just until incorporated and you have a homogenous dough, about 30 seconds. Form the dough into a flattened circle and wrap it in plastic wrap. Refrigerate for 1 hour, minimum.

Line 2 half sheet pans with silicone baking mats. Mark up and cut out a 19-centimeter (7.5-in) square template from poster board or cardboard.

Roll out 200 grams of the tart dough to a thickness of 0.5 centimeter (0.2 in) and slightly larger than the template. Cut a square from the dough, using the template as a guide, and place it on one of the half sheet pans. Add the leftover dough scraps to the unrolled dough. Roll out a second square the same way and place it on the other pan. Refrigerate for at least 20 minutes.

Preheat the oven to 350°F (175°C). Bake until the edges are golden brown and the center looks dry, 15 to 18 minutes. Allow to cool completely.

PARLOR TRICK! To create perfectly straight edges after baking, place the squares on a thick cutting board. Let the square hang a bit over the edge of the board and file the square's sides straight and flat with a plane zester. Repeat for all sides leaving an 18-centimeter (7-in) perfect square.

CRAQUELIN

42 g unsalted butter

50 g brown sugar

50 g all-purpose flour

Red, green, yellow, blue food coloring, as desired

Mix the butter and brown sugar in the bowl of the stand mixer fitted with the paddle attachment on medium speed until smooth, about 2 minutes. Add the flour and mix on low speed until sandy, about 1 minute. Squeeze the mixture in your hands until it sticks together, then divide the dough into 4 parts. Wearing disposable gloves, knead a different color into each portion on a silicone baking mat.

Roll each color dough between 2 pieces of parchment to about the thickness of a credit card. Peel back the top piece of parchment. If it sticks, place it in the freezer for 10 minutes. Cut 15 (3 centimeter [1 in]-diameter) circles from each color of craquelin. Leave the circles in place, place the parchment back on top and place the craquelin in the freezer until ready to use for easier handling.

PÂTE À CHOUX

65 g milk

65 g water

3 g salt

6 g sugar

65 g unsalted butter

73 g bread flour, sifted

132 g eggs

Preheat the oven to 350°F (175°C). Line 2 half sheet pans with silicone baking mats.

In a medium saucepan, warm the milk, water, salt, sugar and butter over medium heat, stirring occasionally, until the butter is melted, about 3 minutes. Then, bring the mixture to a boil. Remove the pan from the heat, add all the flour at once and stir with a wooden spoon. Return the pan to the stove and continue to stir until all the liquid is absorbed and the mixture comes together. Once you see a film of dough on the bottom of the pan and the mixture starts to pull away from the sides and roll toward the middle, about 10 seconds, remove it from the heat. Transfer the mixture to the bowl of the stand mixer fitted with the paddle attachment. Mix on low speed for 1 minute to cool slightly.

In a small bowl, lightly mix the eggs to break up the yolks. Add about a fifth of the eggs to the warm batter and mix on medium speed until they are completely absorbed, about 30 seconds. Add another fifth and allow to incorporate. Continue to add eggs little by little until the batter starts to look glossy and to loosen up, scraping the bottom of the bowl often.

Before all the eggs are added, test the batter by running your finger through it to create a trough. If the tough stays stiff, add more eggs. If the trough slowly moves back inward, but doesn't close completely, stop. This step is crucial, as it will affect its ability to rise in the oven. Err on the side of less egg, as with too much egg your choux may end up flat.

Place the dough in a piping bag fitted with a 1-centimeter (0.5-in) open piping tip. Pipe 60 cream puffs, each about 2.5 centimeters (1 in) in diameter, onto the half sheet pans.

Remove the craquelin from the freezer. Turn the parchment sheets upside down and peel back the top sheet. Using a small offset spatula, loosen the craquelin from the paper and lift it up. Place the craquelin circles on top of the cream puffs, pressing gently just until they stick.

Bake for about 25 minutes. To test for doneness, pick up a puff and see whether it is golden brown on the bottom. To preserve the color, you don't want to brown the tops. Remove the puffs from the sheet pan and place on a wire rack to cool. The finished puffs should be 3.5 centimeters (1.4 in) after baking.

MINT CRÈME LÉGÈRE

½ vanilla bean

325 g milk

4 g fresh mint leaves

80 g sugar

26 g cornstarch

65 g egg yolks

16 g unsalted butter

120 g heavy cream

Cut the vanilla bean in half again lengthwise. Scrape out the seeds and place them and the pod in a saucepan along with the milk. Bring the milk to a boil, then turn off the heat and add the mint. Cover and infuse for 15 minutes. Strain the milk and discard the vanilla bean and mint.

In a medium, microwave-safe bowl, combine the infused milk, sugar, cornstarch, egg yolks and butter. Blend them with an immersion blender and then place the bowl in the microwave. Cook on high until the top and sides of the milk mixture are set and jiggle like Jell-O when you shake the bowl, 1½ to 2 minutes. The center will still be a bit liquid and the sides almost curdled. With a clean immersion blender, mix the milk mixture to combine, scrape the sides of the bowl and continue blending in the center and also just at the surface until smooth. Cover the surface with plastic wrap and refrigerate.

In the bowl of a stand mixer fitted with the whisk attachment, whisk the cream to soft peak. When the mint pastry cream mixture is cool, transfer it a separate bowl of the stand mixer fitted with the paddle attachment and soften it on high speed, about 30 seconds. Fold in the whipped cream with a spatula.

ASSEMBLY

70 g banana slices

70 g raspberries

70 g blueberries

Fresh mint, as needed

Select 41 of the best-looking cream puffs. Place the mint crème légère in a piping bag tightly fitted with a small round pastry tip. Pierce the bottom of the puffs with the tip and pipe to fill.

Place one of the tart squares on a cake board or platter. Arrange 16 cream puffs, alternating colors, along the edge of the tart square. Pipe the center with a layer of crème légère. Top with the banana slices and raspberries. Cover with more crème légère.

Top with the second tart square. Arrange the remaining 25 filled cream puffs, alternating colors, in a grid on top. Sprinkle the blueberries around the top to hide any gaps in between the cream puffs. Garnish with a sprig of fresh mint. Serve the same day as assembled.

CHOCOLATE PANDEMONIUM

DIFFICULTY:

Can you handle it?

You know what they say (or maybe it's just what I say), you can't trust anyone who insists he or she doesn't like chocolate. Here's one for the diehard chocolate fan—chocolate mousse three ways, chocolate ganache and chocolate meringue. It is recommended you serve this dessert within a few hours of creating the meringue nest, so the nest remains crisp.

For this recipe we used two Silikomart "Eclipse" molds (see Sources, page 199). Alternatively, you can build the mousse in two 15-centimeter (6-in) wide, 7.5-centimeters (3-in) high cake rings lined with acetate.

This entremet was also sprayed while frozen with chocolate from a paint sprayer, to give it a unique velvet presentation (see Technique, page 190). If you do not have a paint sprayer, you could also cover it with a liquid chocolate glaze (see The Royale, page 133).

YIELD: 16 servings

CHOCOLATE MERINGUE

16 g dark alkalized cocoa powder

66 g powdered sugar

80 g egg whites

66 g sugar

Preheat the oven to 275°F (135°C). Place a silicone baking mat on a half sheet pan.

Sift the cocoa powder and the powdered sugar into a large bowl. Prepare a French meringue (see page 191) with the egg whites and granulated sugar, whisking to very stiff peak. Since there is a large ratio of sugar to egg whites in this recipe, you do not need to worry about overwhisking your meringue. Just make sure it is stiff. Fold the meringue into the cocoa mixture just until combined.

Place the meringue in a piping bag fitted with a 1-centimeter (0.5-in) open piping tip. Pipe lines of meringue across the baking mat lengthwise. Place in the oven to dry for 1 hour.

CHOCOLATE GANACHE

275 g heavy cream

275 g dark chocolate

80 g egg yolks

Place 2 (15-centimeter [6-in]) cake rings on a half sheet pan and line them with acetate.

Bring the cream to a boil while you melt the chocolate on low in the microwave, stirring often. Slowly whisk the cream into the yolks. Pour one-third of the cream into the chocolate. Whisk vigorously in one section of the bowl. Once that section starts to emulsify and look glossy, start whisking in larger and larger circles until all the chocolate is incorporated. Add the next third of the cream and repeat the same procedure, followed by the last third of cream. The ganache should be glossy and smooth.

Pour 200 grams of the ganache in each cake ring. Reserve the rest at room temperature. Break 50 grams of the meringue into 2.5-centimeter (1 in) pieces. Sink 25 grams of meringue into each of the ganache rings. Freeze until ready to assemble.

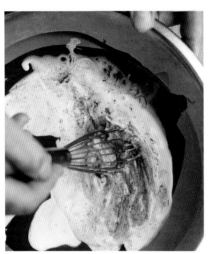  

Create a smooth emusion with the chocolate and cream before adding more cream (see Techniques, page 190).

CHOCOLATE MOUSSE TRIO

710 g heavy cream

170 g egg yolks

125 g honey

160 g dark chocolate

230 g white chocolate

185 g milk chocolate

Place 2 Silikomart "Eclipse" molds on a half sheet pan. In the bowl of a stand mixer fitted with the whisk attachment, whisk the cream to very soft peak and allow it to come to room temperature. Before using, make sure the cream is still at very soft peak as sometimes a liquid portion will sink out to the bottom of the bowl. If that happens, whisk it by hand very briefly until it comes back together.

Place the egg yolks in a separate mixer bowl. Bring the honey to a full boil. While whisking on low speed, pour the hot honey down the side of the bowl, being careful not to let it hit the whisk. Increase the speed to high and whisk until the bottom of the bowl is no longer warm, about 5 minutes. The cooled egg mixture, known as the pâte à bombe in French pastry-making, should be pale and thick.

(continued)

CHOCOLATE MOUSSE TRIO (CONTINUED)

Three mousses will be made, one with each of the different chocolates. Divide the cream (230 g each) among 3 small bowls, and the pâte à bombe (80 g each) among 3 additional bowls.

Melt the dark chocolate in the microwave on low power. Place 80 grams of pâte à bombe in a large bowl. Fold in 230 grams of cream. Pour the dark chocolate in a small pile in a corner of the bowl, making sure to scrape all the chocolate into the bowl. Very quickly fold the chocolate into the cream and pâte à bombe.

Temperature and speed is of utmost importance. If the melted chocolates set up before the mousse is mixed entirely, it will result in a mousse with chocolate pieces floating in it as well as a mousse lacking the chocolate flavor and strength it should have. For best results, make sure the cream is whisked to very soft peak and has little to no chill on it. Make sure the chocolate is quite warm (but not hot). Finally, when folding in the chocolate do it as quickly as possible. Don't forget to turn the bowl as you fold.

Pour half of the dark chocolate mousse in each mold and smooth with a small offset spatula. Next, prepare the white chocolate mousse in the same manner and add a layer to each mold. Freeze for 15 minutes. Prepare the final milk chocolate mousse in the same manner and fill the molds. Freeze overnight.

CHOCOLATE SPRAY

200 g cocoa butter

200 g dark chocolate

In a microwave-safe bowl, combine the cocoa butter and chocolate and microwave on low, stirring very often, until melted. Use immediately (see Assembly).

ASSEMBLY

15 g heavy cream

Powdered sugar, as needed

Silver leaf, as needed

> PARLOR TRICK! If your meringue absorbs humidity and becomes soft, place it in a 300°F (150°C) oven for 10 minutes. Allow to cool and then build your nest.

Unmold the ganache and place on a wire rack. Unmold the mousse disk and center it on top of the ganache, dark-chocolate-mousse-side down. Place the rack in the freezer. Place an empty cardboard box on the counter, open side facing you. Prepare the chocolate spray and a paint sprayer (see Techniques, page 190). When the chocolate spray is 95°F (35°C), strain it into the sprayer. Remove the first entremet and place it the box. Spray the mousse and base with a thin layer of chocolate, turning the wire rack as you go to cover all sides and the top. Repeat with a second layer, making sure all sides are covered and you can no longer see the mousse layers. Repeat with the second entremet.

Move the entremets to larger cake boards or platters, using a large offset spatula. Warm the reserved ganache on the lowest setting in the microwave just until it starts to melt, about 5 to 10 seconds. Add 15 grams of cold cream and whisk until smooth. Pipe the ganache under the mousse and around the sprayed ganache base. Dust small pieces of meringue with powdered sugar and stick them to the ganache, creating a nest. Place a few pieces of meringue on top of the mousse and top with silver leaf.

BYE, BYE PUMPKIN PIE

DIFFICULTY: 🍔 🍔 🍔

This is so much better!

Taking the flavors of a traditional pumpkin pie, lightening the texture, adding some chocolate,
a touch of caramel and spicing things up with some garam masala pecans . . . bam!
Way sexier, way more delicious.

For this recipe, you will need a 20-centimeter (8-in) metal cake ring,
5 centimeters (2 in) in height, and acetate.

YIELD: 12 servings

JOCONDE BISCUIT

65 g powdered sugar

36 g pastry flour

65 g blanched almond meal

100 g eggs

120 g egg whites

30 g sugar, plus more for dusting

15 g unsalted butter, melted

50 g pepitas

Preheat the oven to 425°F (220°C). Line a half sheet pan with a silicone baking mat.

Sift the powdered sugar and flour into the bowl of a stand mixer fitted with the paddle attachment. Add the almond meal and stir to combine. Add the whole eggs and beat on high speed until the batter is light and fluffy, about 4 minutes. Transfer this mixture to a larger bowl and set aside.

Prepare a French meringue (see page 191) with the egg whites and granulated sugar, whisking to soft peak. Do not overwhisk, or else the meringue will become crumbly and not incorporate into the batter well. Very gently, fold half of the meringue into the almond mixture, followed by the butter and then the remaining meringue.

Pour the batter on the silicone mat and spread with a large offset spatula, making sure you have an even thickness across the pan. Sprinkle the pepitas over the cake. Bake for 10 to 12 minutes, rotating once after 6 minutes. The cake is done when the top springs back and is dry to the touch and just barely starting to brown on the top. If overcooked, the cake will become crunchy toward the edges or in shallow spots. Allow to cool.

CHOCOLATE ALMOND CAKE

15 g unsalted butter

50 g dark chocolate

32 g all-purpose flour

15 g powdered sugar

15 g almond meal

30 g honey

40 g egg yolks

75 g egg whites

18 g brown sugar

Preheat the oven to 375°F (190°C). Place a 20-centimeter (8-in) metal cake ring on a half sheet pan lined with a silicone mat.

In a small microwave-safe bowl, melt together the butter and the chocolate in the microwave on low, stirring often.

Sift the flour and powdered sugar into the bowl of the stand mixer fitted with the whisk attachment. Add the almond meal, honey and egg yolks and whisk on high speed until pale, about 2 minutes. Transfer this mixture to a larger bowl and set aside.

Prepare a French meringue (see page 191) with the egg whites and brown sugar, whisking to stiff peak. Take one-fourth of the meringue and stir it into the yolk mixture. This will loosen up the mixture and allow the rest of the meringue to incorporate easier. Fold in half of the remaining meringue, and then the final half. Fold in the chocolate and butter.

Pour into the cake ring and spread evenly with a small offset spatula. Bake until dry to the touch and just barely firm, about 12 to 14 minutes.

FLEUR DE SEL CARAMEL

85 g heavy cream

110 g sugar

10 g unsalted butter

1 g (¼ tsp) fleur de sel sea salt

In a small saucepan, bring the cream to a simmer and set aside.

In a large saucepan, heat one-fourth of the sugar over medium heat. When you see the edges start to melt, after about 1 minute, stir briefly with a wooden spoon and allow the edges to melt again. Stir again and repeat until all the sugar is melted, about another minute. It will have a light, opaque caramel color. Add the rest of the sugar, one-fourth at a time, and follow the same procedure.

Right when you have a deep caramel color, add the hot cream little by little, batting the rising foam back and forth with your spoon until it subsides. Then, add more cream. Strain into a small bowl. Add the butter and stir to melt. Stir in the fleur de sel and allow to cool.

SPICED PECANS

75 g pecans

4 g (2 tsp) garam masala

1.5 g (½ tsp) salt

50 g brown sugar

25 g unsalted butter, melted

Preheat the oven to 300°F (150°C). In a small bowl, combine the pecans, garam masala, salt and brown sugar. Add the melted butter and stir to coat. Pour, in a single layer, onto a sheet pan and toast until light brown and fragrant, about 10 to 12 minutes.

PUMPKIN BAVAROIS

7 g powdered gelatin

35 g cold water

175 g canned pumpkin

75 g milk

100 g sugar

30 g egg yolks

1 g (½ tsp) ground cinnamon

0.5 g (¼ tsp) ground ginger

0.5 g (¼ tsp) ground cloves

300 g heavy cream

In a small bowl, combine the gelatin with the cold water and stir well to dissolve. Let it sit for 5 minutes to bloom.

Place a strainer over a medium bowl and set aside. In a small saucepan, combine the pumpkin, milk, sugar, yolks and spices and blend them with an immersion blender. Heat the pumpkin mixture over low heat, stirring constantly with a heat-safe rubber spatula. When the mixture reaches to 82°C (180°F), immediately strain into the prepared bowl. Add the gelatin and stir to melt. Allow to cool to 104°F (40°C).

In the bowl of a stand mixer fitted with the whisk attachment, whisk the cream to soft peak. Stir one-third of the cream into the cooled pumpkin mixture. Fold in the remaining cream. Use immediately (see Assembly, page 123).

APRICOT GLAZE

275 g apricot jelly, without pulp

Orange food coloring, as desired

Gold dust, as desired

In a small saucepan, blend all the glaze ingredients together with an immersion blender. Bring it to a boil and then cool to 122°F (50°C). Blend again and use immediately (see Assembly, page 123).

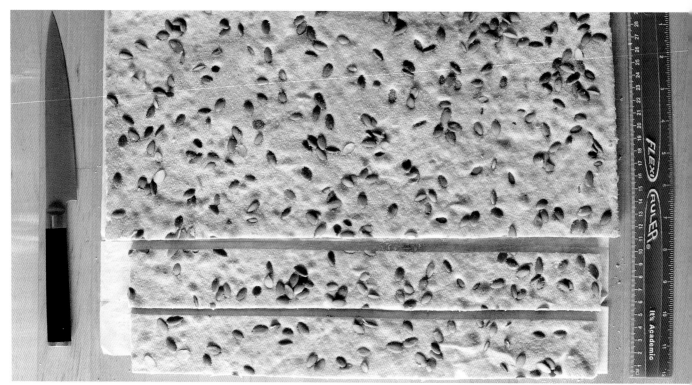

Cut the joconde cake just slightly narrower than the height of your cake ring.

Cut the joconde cake longer than needed. Then push the ends back until they fit together snugly.

ASSEMBLY

Macarons (see Macarons, page 166), optional

Sugar, for dusting

If making the macarons for décor, use one-third of the recipe without the poppy seeds and color them orange instead of yellow. Only a few macarons are used for decoration, but they do make a statement. You could also leave them off and decorate with more pepitas.

Lightly dust the joconde cake top with granulated sugar so it will not stick when unmolding. Cut around the edges to break the cake away from the sides of the pan. Place a piece of parchment over the cake and flip it upside down. Remove the silicone mat slowly, starting at one corner and pulling the mat not up, but almost parallel to the mat itself in the opposite direction. If the cake is sticking or breaking, place it in the freezer and chill for 15 minutes, then try again.

With the cake horizontal in front of you, trim the bottom so you have a clean, straight edge. Make a parallel cut 4.5 centimeters (1.75 in) above the edge. Then, make another the same distance above, that so you have 2 strips of cake the same width. Trim the ends of the strips. Then line the cake ring with acetate and place it on a half sheet pan lined with parchment.

Place 1 strip of cake against the inside of the mold, design facing the ring. Line up the ends of the first and second strips of cake in the mold and roll the cake around the ring until they overlap. Cut the second strip, leaving about a 2.5-centimeter (1-in) overlap (page 122). Then, push the cake ends back until they fit together and the cake is nice and snug all the way around, leaving no gap or overlap.

Unmold the chocolate almond cake. Trim a small amount off the sides so it will fit in the lined cake ring and place it in the bottom. Top the cake with the caramel, followed by the pecans.

Prepare the pumpkin bavarois. Fill the cake ring with the pumpkin bavarois and level off with an offset spatula. Freeze overnight.

Prepare the apricot glaze. Pour enough of the apricot glaze onto the cake, still in the cake ring, to cover the top. Place the cake back in the freezer set up, about 30 minutes. Slide the cake ring off the dessert and then peel off the acetate. Decorate with macarons or as desired.

WHEN LIFE GIVES YOU LEMONS . . .

DIFFICULTY:

. . . make dessert.

This entremet packs bold flavors with very little effort or difficulty, as we show you how to make lemon curd in the microwave. Who's got all that time for stirring? We revisit our sweet tart dough recipe for a crunchy base.

For this recipe, two Silikomart individual "Jr. Pillow" molds were used (see Sources, page 199). You can also put the mousse in a 20-centimeter (8-in) cake ring lined with acetate, add the raspberry gelée and candied lemon to that and cut the base into a 22-centimeter (9-in) circle.

YIELD: 16 servings

SWEET TART DOUGH

50 g egg yolks

2.5 g (½ tsp) vanilla extract

155 g all-purpose flour, plus more for rolling and baking

Pinch of salt

70 g powdered sugar

120 g unsalted butter, cold

In a small bowl, whisk together the egg yolks and vanilla and set aside. Sift the flour, salt and sugar into the bowl of a stand mixer fitted with the paddle attachment and combine on low speed. Cut the butter into 1-centimeter (0.5-in) cubes and add it to the bowl. Continue to mix on low speed until the mixture resembles coarse sand, about 5 minutes. Do not overmix the dry ingredients with the butter. If the mixture starts to stick together, it will not absorb the eggs and it will be very sticky and hard to roll. Add the egg yolk mixture and mix just until incorporated and you have a homogenous dough, about 30 seconds. Form the dough into a flattened circle and wrap it in plastic wrap. Refrigerate for 1 hour, minimum.

RASPBERRY GELÉE

100 g raspberry puree

70 g sugar

In a very small saucepan, combine the puree and sugar and bring to a simmer. Simmer enough to slightly thicken the mixture, about 3 minutes. The cooking time will depend on the size of your saucepan, as a larger surface area will evaporate and thicken faster. To test the thickness, place a few drops on the back of a frozen spoon. The mixture should not run off. Set aside at room temperature. Once cool, the consistency should be thicker but still a bit runny.

LEMON CURD

200 g sugar

140 g fresh lemon juice

100 g egg yolks

80 g eggs

Pinch of salt

50 g unsalted butter, soft

In a medium, microwave-safe bowl, combine all the lemon curd ingredients and blend with an immersion blender. Place the bowl in the microwave and clean the immersion blender.

Cook on high until the mixture coats the back of a spoon. Check the curd after 2 minutes and every 30 seconds after. Every time you check, first blend with a clean immersion blender, as the mixture will not look smooth (but it's fine; trust me!). When you draw your finger through the curd while holding the spoon vertically (its edge facing up), the curd should not move. Once finished, reserve 100 grams to hold at room temperature and refrigerate the rest.

The mixture will not look smooth (left). When you draw your finger through the curd, it shouldn't move (right).

LEMON MOUSSE

12 g powdered gelatin

60 g cold water

480 g heavy cream

410 g lemon curd, cold, plus 100 g at room temperature

50 g fresh lemon juice

In a medium, microwave-safe bowl, combine the gelatin with the cold water and stir well to dissolve. Let it sit for 5 minutes to bloom.

In the bowl of the stand mixer fitted with the whisk attachment, whisk the cream to soft peak. Place the cold 410 grams of lemon curd in a large bowl and whisk by hand until smooth.

Melt the gelatin on low in the microwave. Swirl the bowl to stir the gelatin every 30 seconds, until it is completely melted. While whisking continually, add the lemon juice to the gelatin, followed by the 100 grams of room-temperature lemon curd. Pour this into the cold lemon curd and fold quickly with a whisk. Fold in half of the whipped cream, followed by the second half. Use immediately (see Assembly).

ASSEMBLY

30 g candied lemons

No melt/donut sugar, as needed

16 pieces fresh raspberries

Lemon zest, as needed

Prepare the mousse as instructed. Pipe the mold cavities three-fourths full with the mousse.

Place the raspberry gelée into a small piping bag fitted with a small open piping tip. With the tip submerged in the mousse, pipe a line through it. Add a few pieces of candied lemon to each cavity. Fill with the remaining mousse and smooth the tops with a small offset spatula. Freeze overnight.

Preheat the oven to 350°F (175°C). Roll the tart dough to a thickness of 0.5 centimeter (0.2 in). Cut out 16 (8 centimeter [3 in]) oval bases with the cutter provided with the mold. If using a 20-centimeter (8-in) cake ring, cut out a 23-centimeter (9-in) circle to use as the base. Bake for 12 to 14 minutes, or until the edges just start to brown.

Unmold the frozen mousse and place it on a wire rack. Tilting the rack, sprinkle the sides and tops with donut sugar. Place each mousse cake on an oval of the sweet tart dough, using an offset spatula. Top each with a fresh raspberry and piece of lemon zest.

DADDY MAC

DIFFICULTY: 🍪 🍪 🍪

Or Mac Daddy? Warm it up, Kris.

The ultimate macaron. Take the much loved macaron and elevate the filling from mere buttercream to a mix of pistachio mousse, poached apricots and white chocolate ganache. The macarons should have a thin shell, chewy interior and the renowned crackled rim called the "foot."

For this recipe, you will need a 15-centimeter (6-in) cake ring and acetate.

YIELD: 12 servings

POACHED APRICOTS

4 apricots

1000 g water

300 g sugar

1 vanilla bean

10 g unsalted butter

Cut the apricots in half and remove the pits.

In a wide, shallow saucepan, combine the water and sugar and stir. Cut the vanilla bean in half lengthwise. Scrape out the seeds and add them, plus the pod, to the pan.

Bring the sugar mixture to a simmer. Add the apricots, cut side down. Simmer for 5 minutes and then flip over the apricots. Continue to simmer until a knife can pierce the apricots without resistance, about 3 minutes. Transfer the apricots to a half sheet pan lined with paper towels and allow to cool. Wash the vanilla bean and save it for décor.

In a wide skillet, melt the butter over medium heat. Add the apricots, flat side down, and cook for 2 minutes, or until the apricots have a light char on them. Transfer them to the paper towels to cool.

WHITE CHOCOLATE VANILLA CREAM

125 g heavy cream, plus 250 g, cold

½ vanilla bean

125 g white chocolate

Place the cream in a small saucepan. Cut the vanilla bean in half lengthwise. Scrape out the seeds and add them, plus the pod, to the cream. Bring the cream to a boil, then turn off the heat, cover and infuse for 15 minutes. Strain the cream and discard the vanilla bean.

In a medium bowl, melt the chocolate in the microwave on low power. Pour one-third of the cream into the chocolate. Whisk vigorously in the center of the bowl. Once the center starts to emulsify and look glossy, start whisking in larger and larger circles until all the chocolate is incorporated. Add the next third of the cream and repeat the same procedure, followed by the last third of cream. The ganache should be glossy and smooth. Whisk in the cold cream. Refrigerate for 4 or more hours.

PISTACHIO MOUSSE

2 g powdered gelatin

10 g cold water

155 g milk

40 g egg yolk

45 g sugar

18 g cornstarch

15 g pistachio paste

185 g heavy cream

6 halves poached apricots

Place a 15-centimeter (6-in) cake ring on a half sheet pan lined with parchment. Line the ring with acetate.

In a small bowl, combine the gelatin with the cold water and stir well to dissolve. Let sit for 5 minutes to bloom.

Place the milk, egg yolks, sugar, cornstarch and pistachio paste in a small microwave-safe bowl. Blend them with an immersion blender and then place the bowl in the microwave. Cook on high until the top and sides of the pistachio mixture are set and jiggle like Jell-O when you shake the bowl, about 1½ to 2 minutes. The center will still be a bit liquid and the sides almost curdled. With a clean immersion blender, blend the pistachio mixture to combine, scrape the sides of the bowl and continue to blend in the center and also just at the surface until smooth. Stir in the gelatin. Allow to cool to 104°F (40°C), stirring often. Once the required temperature is reached, blend with the immersion blender again.

In the bowl of a stand mixer fitted with the whisk attachment, whisk the cream to soft peak. Fold half of the cream into the pistachio mixture, followed by the second half. Pour the mousse into the cake ring (it will only fill about 4 centimeters [1.5 in] of the ring). Sink 6 apricot halves into the mousse completely, saving 2 of the halves for décor. Level off the mousse with an offset spatula and freeze overnight.

PISTACHIO MACARON

168 g powdered sugar

112 g blanched almond meal

100 g egg whites

50 g granulated sugar

Green food coloring, as desired

10 g pistachios, finely chopped

> **PARLOR TRICK!** Always double-pan macarons when baking, or use a heavy-duty steel pan as they do in France. If you don't, your macarons will have cracked tops.

Preheat the oven to 350°F (175°C). Trace a 20-centimeter (8-in) cake ring on 2 pieces of parchment paper. Put each piece of parchment on 2 double-panned half sheet pans. Top with silicone baking mats.

In a food processor, combine the powdered sugar and the almond meal. Process for 30 seconds to get a more refined almond meal. Sift this mixture into a wide, large bowl and set aside. Prepare a stiff French meringue (see page 191) with the egg whites and granulated sugar. Due to the high proportion of sugar to egg whites, in this recipe you can whisk away with confidence, as there is little risk of overwhisking the meringue. When your meringue is finished, add coloring until the desired shade is reached.

Add all the meringue to the bowl with the almond mixture. Now we start what I call the "Fold, Smear, Smear" technique. Using a plastic bowl scraper, fold the almond meal through and over the meringue once. Then, use the bowl scraper to smear the meringue and almonds against the bowl twice. In addition to incorporating the meringue with the almonds, we are purposely deflating our meringue. Continue to fold once, then smear twice, until your batter just barely moves, like very, very slow lava. I mean so slow you have to really stop and stare at it to see it move.

Place the macaron mixture in a piping bag fitted with a 1.25-centimeter (0.5-in) tip. Pipe a spiral starting from the inside of each template circle, moving to the outside but staying in the borders of the template. Sprinkle each macaron with the chopped pistachios. Space out the pans in the oven and bake for 20 to 25 minutes. If you put a finger on one of the macaron tops and try to wiggle it slightly, it should not move. If it does, bake for another minute or so. Remove the bottom pans and allow the macarons to cool. Once cool, the macarons should have a firm top, soft center and the crackled rim known as the "foot." Freeze the macarons until assembly to make them easier to handle.

ASSEMBLY

Physalis, as desired

Gently flip the silicone mats over and peel them back to remove the macarons. Place a macaron upside down on a cake board or platter. Remove the cake ring and acetate from the pistachio mousse and place it in the center of the macaron.

Remove the white chocolate vanilla cream from the refrigerator and place in the bowl of a stand mixer fitted with the whisk attachment. Whisk on high speed until thick and pipeable, about 1 minute.

Place the white chocolate vanilla cream in a piping bag fitted with a 1-centimeter (0.5-in) open tip. Pipe dollops of cream around the mousse, followed by a second layer of dollops on top. Place the second macaron on top of the mousse and cream. Decorate with the remaining apricot halves, physalis and the reserved vanilla bean.

THE ROYALE

DIFFICULTY: 🍪 🍪 🍪

Fit for a king, or a queen, or you!

This combination of chocolate mousse, crunchy hazelnut and dacquoise is becoming the latest in modern classics on the streets of Paris. I am sure you will love this version (what's not to love about chocolate and hazelnuts?). The buttercream is made with an Italian meringue. Italian meringue is the most difficult meringue but gives the lightest texture and thus is worth the effort.

Try the Royale with cheese—serve with a slice of any soft triple cream cheese, such as a Brillat Savarin, for a complementing texture and contrasting flavor profile. Really. Try it.

For this recipe, you will need three 7.5-centimeter (3-in) silicone demisphere molds with six cavities per mold.

YIELD: 15 servings

ALMOND DACQUOISE

80 g powdered sugar

15 g pastry flour

80 g almond meal

100 g egg whites

65 g granulated sugar

Preheat the oven to 350°F (175°C). Using a pastry cutter, trace 15 (7.5 centimeter [3 in]) circles onto 2 pieces of parchment paper. Flip the sheets over and place them on 2 half sheet pans.

Sift the powdered sugar and flour into a very large bowl. Add the almond meal. Prepare a French meringue (see page 191) with the egg whites and granulated sugar, whisking to stiff peak. Add the meringue to the almond meal mixture. Gently fold the two together. The mixture should be light and fluffy, not runny, when finished.

Using a pastry bag fitted with a 1-centimeter (0.5-in) open pastry tip, pipe the dacquoise into the circles. Start from the center and spiral out to the edge.

Bake until just starting to turn a light golden brown, 16 to 18 minutes total. When cool, the dacquoise should be crisp on the outside but chewy on the inside.

HAZELNUT CRUNCH

40 g milk chocolate

38 g bittersweet chocolate

32 g unsalted butter

150 g unsweetened hazelnut paste

65 g pailleté feuilletine

Line a half sheet pan with a piece of parchment.

In a small, microwave-safe bowl, combine the chocolates and butter and microwave on low, stirring often, just until melted. Stir in the hazelnut paste and the pailleté feuilletine. Pour the mixture onto the parchment and spread it into a 25-centimeter (10-in) square. Place it in the refrigerator to set up. When solid, cut out 15 (6.5 centimeter [2.5 in]) circles and reserve in the refrigerator.

> NOTE: Pailleté feuilletine is essentially very thin, flaky dehydrated crepes. Its main purpose is to give texture. If you cannot find it, substitute crushed fortune cookies or corn flakes.

HAZELNUT BUTTERCREAM

225 g sugar, divided

220 g water

68 g egg whites

225 g unsalted butter, softened

60 g unsweetened hazelnut paste

In a small saucepan, combine 170 grams of the sugar and the water and stir. Place a thermometer in the pan and turn on the heat to medium. Dip a pastry brush in a glass of water and then use it to wipe down any sugar crystals sticking to the insides of the pan above the water. Carefully watch the temperature. You will cook the sugar to a range of 245 to 250°F (118 to 121°C).

Place the egg whites in the bowl of the stand mixer fitted with the whisk attachment. When your sugar reaches 221°F (105°C), start whisking the egg whites on high speed. When they are foamy, add the remaining 55 grams of sugar and keep whisking. Now your goal is to bring the egg whites just to stiff peak at the same time your sugar syrup reaches its temperature range. The most important thing to keep in mind is to not overcook the sugar (it will be too hard to incorporate) or overwhip the egg whites (the meringue will collapse). Err on the lower end, if necessary. To help sync the timing, you can always raise or lower your heat (or turn it off completely!) or raise or lower the speed at which you are whisking the eggs.

When your syrup reaches 245 to 250°F (118 to 121°C) and the egg whites are at stiff peak, turn the mixer speed to low. *Slowly* pour the syrup down the side of the bowl and into the meringue, being careful not pour it on the whisk. Once all the syrup is in, continue to whisk the mixture on medium speed until the bottom of the bowl is no longer warm when you touch it, about 10 minutes. Add your softened butter and whisk on medium speed to combine, about 30 seconds. Add the hazelnut paste and whisk just until combined, about 10 seconds. Use at room temperature.

If the bottom of the whisk does not reach the egg whites in the bowl (for example, if you have a 5.7 liter [6 qt] bowl or larger), you can use a towel to prop up one side. Place the towel on the arm of the stand mixer with the bowl resting on top of the towel but still secure to the stand mixer in the back. Do this with the mixer turned off.

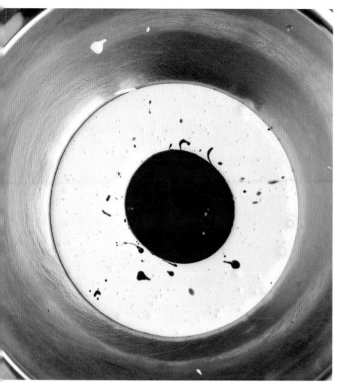

d the chocolate to the pâte à bombe.

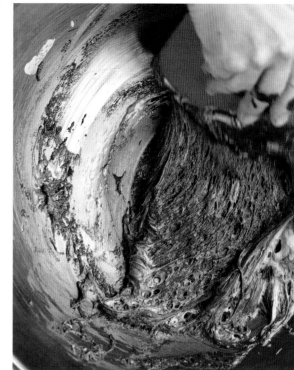

Fold quickly and thoroughly.

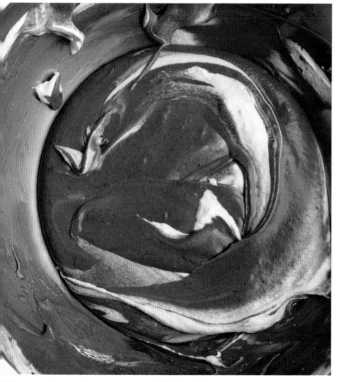

d the room temperature cream, one-third at a time.

The whole mixing process should take 30 seconds or less. Use immediately.

CHOCOLATE GLAZE

190 g heavy cream

230 g water

290 g sugar

95 g dark alkalized cocoa powder

10 g powdered gelatin

50 g cold water

In a large saucepan, combine the cream, water and sugar and bring to a boil. Remove from the heat and whisk in the cocoa powder. Bring the mixture back to a boil and then strain it into a bowl. Allow to cool.

In a small bowl, combine the gelatin with the cold water and stir well to dissolve. Let sit for 5 minutes to bloom.

When the glaze reaches 140°F (60°C), add the gelatin mixture and gently combine with an immersion blender. Refrigerate.

CHOCOLATE MOUSSE

500 g heavy cream

90 g egg yolks

90 g honey

185 g milk chocolate

125 g dark chocolate

In the bowl of a stand mixer fitted with the whisk attachment, whisk the cream to very soft peak and allow it to come to room temperature. Make sure the cream is still at very soft peak just before using, as sometimes a liquid portion will sink out to the bottom of the bowl. If that happens, whisk it by hand very briefly until it comes back together.

Place the egg yolks in a separate mixer bowl. Bring the honey to a full boil. While whisking on low speed, pour the hot honey down the side of the bowl, being careful not to let it hit the whisk. Increase the speed to high and whisk until the bottom of the bowl is no longer warm, about 5 minutes. The cooled egg mixture, known as the pâte à bombe in French pastry-making, should be pale and thick.

Melt the chocolate in the microwave on low, stirring often.

Pour the pâte à bombe into large, shallow bowl. Pour all the warm melted chocolate onto the pâte à bombe. With a bowl scraper, stir the two together very quickly, starting in the center and then incorporating the rest. Once the mixture looks homogenous, quickly stir in one-third of the cream until evenly mixed, then fold in the remaining cream. The whole mixing process should take about 30 seconds or less. Use immediately (see Assembly, page 137).

A note about mixing: The melted chocolate in the recipe will want to set up very quickly. It is imperative that you mix the pâte à bombe and the chocolate together quickly, and then add just one-third of the cream (at room temperature) to incorporate and loosen the chocolate pâte à bombe mixture. The rest of the cream should then incorporate well when added. If your cream is too cold or you do not mix fast enough, the chocolate will set up into small bits in the mousse. This will result in a mousse with chocolate pieces floating in it as well as a mousse lacking the chocolate flavor it should have.

ASSEMBLY

Gold dust, as desired

Prepare the chocolate mousse and pipe it into 15 (7.5 centimeter [3 in]) silicone demisphere molds. Sink a circle of hazelnut crunch into the mousse just below the top of the mold. Smooth off the molds, using an offset spatula. Freeze overnight.

Warm the glaze to 90°F (32°C). Unmold the chocolate mousse domes and place them on a wire rack with a sheet pan underneath. Pour enough glaze over each dome to cover. Using a small offset spatula, carefully pick up the frozen mousse domes and place them on top of the dacquoise circles.

Using the tip of a paring knife, pick up a small amount of gold dust. Blow it off the knife just above the mousse, so it falls onto the glaze.

Place the buttercream in the bowl of the stand mixer fitted with the paddle attachment and beat on high speed until smooth, about 5 minutes if cold. Place the buttercream in a small piping bag fitted with a small star tip. Pipe small teardrops around the base of the dessert, starting on the dacquoise and ending slightly up the side of the mousse.

JEREZ

DIFFICULTY:

Sunshine, flamenco, sherry . . . pack your bags.

Jerez, short for Jerez de la Frontera, is one of three main cities in the south of Spain known for the production of sherry wine. Together with the coastal towns of Sanlúcar de Barrameda and El Puerto de Santa Maria, it forms what is known as the sherry triangle. Grapes for sherry wine are grown throughout the triangle, but the sherry itself must be aged in one of these three towns that make up the angles of the triangle.

Sherry wine comes in many styles from bone dry to lusciously sweet. For this recipe, look for an amontillado sherry, which is nutty and dry, to match the flavors of the hazelnut dacquoise and caramelized pine nuts. The sherry will also have some similar flavors of the dried fruits. (If all you can find is cream sherry, use it! We wouldn't want to deprive you of this deliciousness.) The cinnamon streusel gives a hint of spice and a lot of crunch.

For this recipe, you will need a 20-centimeter (8-in) cake ring, 5 centimeters (2 in) tall, with acetate for the assembly.

We trimmed the sides into a triangle to represent the sherry triangle shape, but it is not necessary.

YIELD: 8 servings

DRIED FRUIT MIX

30 g dried apricots

30 g prunes

30 g candied orange peel

60 g amontillado sherry

Finely chop the dried fruit. Place in a small saucepan, add the sherry and bring the mixture to a simmer. Remove from the heat, cover and allow to sit for at least 30 minutes.

HAZELNUT DACQUOISE

65 g powdered sugar

65 g hazelnut meal

75 g egg whites

25 g granulated sugar

Preheat the oven to 375°F (190°C). Trace a 20-centimeter (8-in) cake ring twice onto a half sheet of parchment. Place the template on a half sheet pan with a silicone baking mat on top.

Sift the powdered sugar into a large bowl and add the hazelnut meal. Prepare a French meringue (see page 191) with the egg whites and granulated sugar, whisking to stiff peak. Add the meringue to the hazelnut mixture and fold to combine.

Using a 1-centimeter (0.4-in) pastry tip, pipe the dacquoise onto the silicone mat in a spiral, starting in the center. Fill the template circles but leave a 1.25-centimeter (0.5-in) space around the edge. Bake until the top is golden brown and slightly firm, about 16 to 18 minutes. When cool, the dacquoise should be crisp on the outside but soft in the middle.

CINNAMON STREUSEL

40 g unsalted butter

32 g brown sugar

32 g almond meal

40 g pastry flour

Pinch of salt

0.5 g (¼ tsp) ground cinnamon

Preheat the oven to 350°F (175°C). Line a half sheet pan with a silicone baking mat.

Mix the butter with the brown sugar in the bowl of a stand mixer fitted with the paddle attachment on medium speed until well combined, about 2 minutes.

Stir the almond meal, flour, salt and cinnamon together and then add them to the butter mixture. Mix on low speed until the dough starts clumping together, about 1 minute. Remove the dough from the bowl and form it into a single mass.

Break off random-shaped pieces about the size of a hazelnut onto the pan in a single layer. Bake until lightly golden brown, about 12 to 14 minutes.

SHERRY MOUSSE

390 g heavy cream

195 g amontillado sherry

108 g sugar

75 g egg yolks

12 g powdered gelatin

60 g cold water

In the bowl of the stand mixer fitted with the whisk attachment, whisk the cream to soft peak and set aside at room temperature in a large bowl.

In a small saucepan, combine the sherry and sugar and warm the mixture over medium heat to dissolve the sugar, about 2 minutes. Place the egg yolks in a medium bowl. Slowly whisk the warm sherry mixture into the eggs. Return the mixture to the saucepan.

Rest a strainer on a separate bowl of the stand mixer still fitted with the whisk attachment. Reheat the sherry mixture over medium heat, stirring constantly with a rubber spatula so the mixture does not stick to the pan. At 180°F (82°C), immediately strain into the prepared bowl. Whisk the mixture on high speed until the bottom of the bowl is no longer warm to the touch and the mixture is light and airy, about 8 minutes.

While the mixture is cooling, in a medium, microwave-safe bowl, combine the gelatin with the cold water and stir well to dissolve. Let sit for 5 minutes to bloom.

Melt the gelatin on low in the microwave. Swirl the bowl to stir the gelatin every 30 seconds, until it is completely melted. Slowly pour one-third of the sherry mixture into the gelatin while whisking quickly. Continue to add the rest of the sherry mixture, now stirring quickly with the whisk. Add half of the cream and stir quickly with the whisk, followed by the second half. Use immediately (see Assembly, page 143).

NOTE: This mousse sets up very quickly. It is important you have all your ingredients and equipment ready before starting to mix it together!

CARAMEL GLAZE

8 g powdered gelatin

40 g cold water

300 g heavy cream

140 g sugar

In a small bowl, combine the gelatin with the cold water and stir well to dissolve. Let it sit for 5 minutes to bloom.

In a small saucepan, bring the cream to a simmer and set aside.

In a large saucepan, cook one-fourth of the sugar over medium heat. When you see the edges start to melt, after about 1 minute, stir briefly with a wooden spoon and allow the edges to melt again. Stir again and repeat until all the sugar is melted, about another minute. It will have a light, opaque caramel color. Add the rest of the sugar, one-fourth at a time, and follow the same procedure.

Right when you have a deep caramel color, add the hot cream little by little, batting the rising foam back and forth with your spoon until it subsides. Then add more cream. Strain into a small bowl. Add the gelatin and stir to melt. Reserve at room temperature.

CARAMELIZED PINE NUTS

50 g sugar

12 g water

80 g pine nuts

Place a silicone baking mat on a half sheet pan.

In a small saucepan, combine the sugar and water. Heat the sugar until it reaches 240°F (116°C). Add the pine nuts and stir with a wooden spoon to coat. Continue to cook over medium heat, stirring about every 5 seconds. The sugar will seize up and crystalize. Then, with time, the sugar will melt again and caramelize. As it starts to caramelize, stir constantly. Once the nuts are fragrant and coated in a golden brown caramel, remove from the heat and pour the nuts onto the silicone mat. Spread out into a single layer and allow to cool.

ASSEMBLY

Line a 20-centimeter (8-in) cake ring with acetate and place on a half sheet pan lined with parchment. Strain the dried fruit.

Prepare the mousse. Place a disk of dacquoise in the bottom of the ring. Top with one-third of the mousse and spread flat. Cover the mousse with the dried fruit and streusel. Add another third of mousse and top with the second disk of dacquoise, pressing down gently to even out the mousse underneath. Use the remaining mousse to fill the ring. Level the top with a large offset spatula. Freeze overnight.

Warm the caramel glaze to 93°F (34°C). Slide the cake ring off the dessert and peel off the acetate. At this point, you can leave the dessert as a circle or cut it into a triangle. If you want to make a triangle shape, cut off 3 sides of the circle, leaving an 18-centimeter (7-in) equilateral triangle. Place the dessert on a wire rack over a half sheet pan. With the glaze at the correct temperature, quickly and generously pour it over the frozen dessert, making sure all the sides are covered.

Using a large offset spatula, push the glaze once to level off, letting the excess fall over the edges. Clean the offset spatula and use it to lift up the cake slightly. Move it in small circular motions against the rack to remove any excess glaze from the bottom. Place it on a cake board or platter.

Press the caramelized pine nuts against the sides of the dessert and add a few on the top.

NOT YOUR GRANDMOTHER'S BÛCHE DE NOËL

DIFFICULTY:

Nor Martha Stewart's, for that matter.

We've all seen the bûches de noël attempting to disguise themselves as pieces of wood (page 31). They are cute, sure. But the modern bûche is sexy.

The bûche de noël here is soft and silky, with a base of chocolate mousse hiding a festive cannoli filling and brandied cherries. There is a bit of chocolate cake along the bottom to hold everything together, and a brilliantly shiny chocolate glaze covering the top.

For this recipe, you will need a bûche de noël mold 50 centimeters (20 in) long and 9 centimeters (3.5 in) wide and a demisphere polycarbonate mold to make the ornaments. If you do not want to invest in a bûche de noël mold, you could make your own with a poster tube from the post office (see Assembly, page 149).

YIELD: 10 servings (2 bûches de noël of 5 servings each)

CHOCOLATE BISCUIT

120 g egg yolks

185 g egg whites

68 g sugar

50 g cocoa powder

Preheat the oven to 350°F (175°C). Line a half sheet pan with a silicone baking mat.

In the bowl of a stand mixer fitted with the whisk attachment, whisk the egg yolks on high speed until they are thick and pale in color, about 5 minutes. Transfer the yolks to a bigger bowl with a larger surface area on top.

Prepare a French meringue (see page 191) with the egg whites and sugar, whisking to soft peak. Add half of the meringue to the yolks and gently fold to combine. Sift half of the cocoa onto the batter in a thin layer covering the top. Gently fold the cocoa into the batter. Repeat with the rest of the meringue and then the rest of the cocoa, being careful not to overmix. Ideally, if you have a helper in the kitchen, have the person continually sift the cocoa over the batter while you continually fold.

Spread evenly onto the half sheet pan, using an offset spatula. Bake until cake is dry to the touch and feels firm, about 12 to 14 minutes.

CANNOLI FILLING

2 g (scant ½ tsp) powdered gelatin

10 g cold water

50 g cream cheese

265 g ricotta cheese

50 g powdered sugar

1 g (½ tsp) ground cinnamon

2 g orange zest

5 g (1 tsp) vanilla extract

25 g dark chocolate, finely chopped

10 g Cointreau

In a large, microwave-safe bowl, combine the gelatin with the cold water and stir well to dissolve. Let it sit for 5 minutes to bloom.

In the bowl of the stand mixer fitted with the paddle attachment, mix together the cream cheese and ricotta on medium speed until smooth, about 30 seconds. Sift the powdered sugar and add it, plus all the remaining filling ingredients, except the Cointreau and gelatin, to the cheese mixture. Mix until combined, about 20 seconds.

Melt the gelatin on low in the microwave. Swirl the bowl to stir the gelatin every 30 seconds, until it is completely melted. While stirring, add the Cointreau to the gelatin. Then add a fourth of the cheese mixture, continuing to stir. Add the remaining cheese mixture, stir to combine and place in the refrigerator.

CHOCOLATE GLAZE

95 g heavy cream

115 g water

145 g sugar

48 g cocoa powder

5 g powdered gelatin

25 g cold water

In a medium saucepan, combine the cream, water and sugar and bring to a boil. Remove from the heat and whisk in the cocoa powder. Bring the mixture back to a boil and then strain it into a bowl. Allow to cool.

In a small bowl, combine the gelatin with the cold water and stir well to dissolve. Let it sit for 5 minutes to bloom.

When the glaze reaches 140°F (60°C), add the gelatin mixture and gently combine with an immersion blender. Refrigerate.

CHOCOLATE MOUSSE

500 g heavy cream

90 g egg yolks

90 g honey

185 g milk chocolate

125 g dark chocolate

In the bowl of the stand mixer fitted with the whisk attachment, whisk the cream to very soft peak and allow it to come to room temperature. Make sure the cream is still at very soft peak just before using, as sometimes a liquid portion will sink out to the bottom of the bowl. If that happens, whisk it by hand very briefly until it comes back together.

Place the egg yolks in a separate mixer bowl. Bring the honey to a full boil. While whisking on low speed, pour the hot honey down the side of the bowl being careful not to let it hit the whisk. Increase the speed to high and whisk until the bottom of the bowl is no longer warm, about 5 minutes. The cooled egg mixture, known as the pâte à bombe in French pastry-making, should be pale and thick.

Melt the chocolate in the microwave on low, stirring often.

Pour the pâte à bombe into a bowl large, shallow bowl. Pour all the melted chocolate onto the pâte à bombe. With a bowl scraper, stir the two together very quickly, starting in the center and then incorporating the rest. Once the mixture looks homogenous, quickly stir in one-third of the cream until evenly mixed, then fold in the remaining cream. The whole mixing process should take about 30 seconds or less. Use immediately (see Assembly, page 149).

A note about mixing: The melted chocolate in the recipe will want to set up very quickly. It is imperative that you mix the pâte à bombe and the chocolate together quickly, and then add just one-third of the cream (at room temperature) to incorporate and loosen the chocolate pâte à bombe mixture. The rest of the cream should then incorporate well when added. If your cream is too cold or you do not mix fast enough, the chocolate will set up into small bits in the mousse. This will result in a mousse with chocolate pieces floating in it as well as a mousse lacking the chocolate flavor it should have.

CHOCOLATE ORNAMENTS

Green cocoa butter, as needed

Gold luster dust, as needed

Red cocoa butter, as needed

800 g dark chocolate

Warm the green and red colored cocoa butters to 90 to 93°F (32 to 34°C). Wearing latex gloves, use your finger to smear a swirl of green cocoa butter in the cavities of demisphere polycarbonate molds. Once the cocoa butter is dry, about 3 minutes, smear each cavity with some of the gold luster dust. Follow with a smear of red cocoa butter.

Temper the chocolate in the microwave (see Techniques, page 190). Pour the chocolate into the mold to fill all the cavities. Tap the mold on the edge of the counter fast and vigorously for a few seconds to release any air bubbles. Flip the mold upside down, holding it over a piece of parchment. Tap the side of the mold with a wide metal scraper to get rid of the excess chocolate. Scrape the top of the mold smooth and place it upside down on a clean piece of parchment.

After 1 minute, lift up the mold and scrape the top clean with the metal scraper. Place it right side up in the refrigerator to chill for 5 minutes, to set the chocolate. Repeat with the second mold. Remove the molds from the refrigerator and let sit for another 10 minutes.

Slide half of the demispheres out of the mold. Heat the metal scraper with a propane torch. Holding the demisphere flat on the surface of the scraper, melt the edges. Piece the melted edges together with the edges of one of the demispheres still in the mold. Continue until all the spheres are complete.

> PARLOR TRICK! If you have a pancake griddle, you can turn that on low and use it to melt the ornament edges. This way you won't have to keep reheating the metal scraper.

ASSEMBLY

200 g brandied cherries

40 g pistachios, finely chopped

Strain the cherries and reserve the juice.

Line a bûche de noël mold with a piece of parchment. The parchment should cover the whole interior and hang over the sides. Unmold the chocolate cake and cut 8-centimeter (3-in) strips from it. You will need enough 8-centimeter (3-in)-wide cake strips to cover the bottom of the mold, or 50 centimeters (20 in) total. If you made your own mold (see Parlor Trick!), cut the cake into narrower 6.25-centimeter (2.5-in) strips.

Prepare the chocolate mousse and pipe it in the mold to fill halfway. With a 1.5-centimeter (0.6-in) open piping tip, pipe a line of cannoli filling lengthwise down the center. Place the cherries, one by one, touching each other, in a line on top of the cannoli filling. Add more mousse to fill the mold 2 centimeters (0.75 in) from the top. Lay the cake on top of the mousse and press it gently until it is just below the top of the mold. Brush the cake with the reserved juice from the cherries. Freeze overnight.

Remove the bûche from the mold by lifting up the edges of parchment paper. If the bûche sticks on the ends, warm them with a propane torch or simply wait a few minutes for the edges to thaw. If you made your own mold, remove the plastic wrap on the ends and slide the bûche out of the tube. Remove the parchment and place the bûche flat side down on a clean piece of parchment.

Warm the chocolate glaze in the microwave to 90°F (32°C) and pour it over the entire bûche. Using a large offset spatula and your hand as a guide, lift up the bûche and place it on a large, clean piece of parchment. Cut the bûche in half and then trim the ends that have glaze on them. Press chopped pistachios 2 centimeters (1 in) up the sides. Using a large offset spatula, lift each bûche off the parchment and place them onto cake boards or platters. Top the bûche with the chocolate ornaments.

PARLOR TRICK! Purchase a 7.5-centimeter (3-in)-diameter poster tube from the post office to make your own bûche de noël mold. Using a utility knife, cut the tube down to 50 centimeters (20 in) long. Then, draw a straight line down the tube from one end to the other. From this line, measure 7.5 centimeters (3 in) around the circumference and draw a parallel line down the tube. Cut out this section with the utility knife. Tape plastic wrap on the ends to close them off. A bûche de noël mold is curved with straight sides toward the bottom. This makeshift mold will have a bit of curvature on the bottom. When you line it with parchment, crease the parchment back at the edges so it does not get in your way when filling.

MOULIN ROUGE

DIFFICULTY: 🍪 🍪 🌙

You like strawberries. And I like you.

A show-stopping cabaret of flavors starring strawberry as the lead with coconut and black pepper in supporting roles. Incredibly bright with a silky textured mousse and tender meringue.

The décor on the cake is made with a pastry stencil. If you don't have a pastry stencil, you can brush or pipe the tuile on the baking mat in a design of your choice.

For this recipe, you will need a 20-centimeter (8-in) cake ring, 5 centimeters (2 in) tall, acetate and a pastry stencil.

YIELD: 8 servings

TUILE DÉCOR

50 g unsalted butter

56 g powdered sugar

60 g egg whites

56 g pastry flour

Red food coloring, as desired

Pan release spray

In the bowl of a stand mixer fitted with the paddle attachment, mix the butter and powdered sugar on high speed until light and fluffy, about 2 minutes. Add the whites in 4 parts, scraping down the bowl after each addition. Add the flour and mix on low speed until just combined, about 30 seconds. Add the coloring.

On a very flat surface, spray a silicone baking mat with pan release and then spread it all over the mat with a paper towel. Lay the stencil flat on the mat. Using a small offset spatula, spread the tuile paste over the stencil to fill in the voids and scrape the top perfectly clean. Carefully lift the far left corner up and toward you, rolling it off the mat without disturbing the design. Slide the mat onto a very flat sheet pan and freeze for 15 minutes.

PARLOR TRICK! The whites will incorporate easier if the butter and powdered sugar are not cold. You can warm the bottom of the bowl slightly with a propane torch to soften the mixture a bit. Just be careful not to melt it.

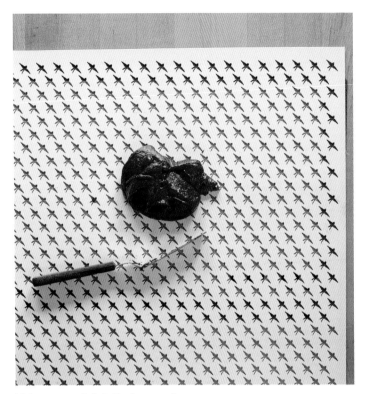

Make sure your tuile batter is very soft.

Smear the tuile batter on a pastry stencil of your choice.

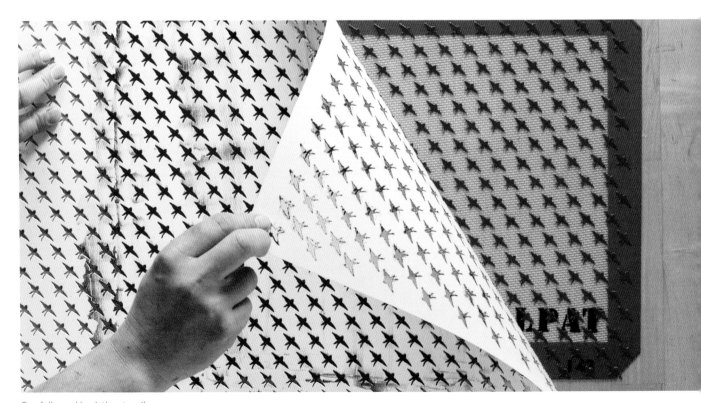

Carefully peel back the stencil.

JOCONDE BISCUIT

65 g powdered sugar

36 g pastry flour

65 g blanched almond meal

100 g eggs

120 g egg whites

30 g granulated sugar, plus more for dusting

15 g unsalted butter, melted

Preheat the oven to 425°F (220°C).

Sift the powdered sugar and flour into the bowl of the stand mixer fitted with the paddle attachment. Add the almond meal and stir to combine. Add the whole eggs and beat on high speed until the batter is light and fluffy, about 4 minutes. Transfer this mixture to a larger bowl and set aside.

Prepare a French meringue (see page 191) with the egg whites and granulated sugar, whisking to soft peak. Do not overwhisk, or else the meringue will become crumbly and not incorporate into the batter well. Very gently, fold half of the meringue into the almond mixture, followed by the butter and then the remaining meringue.

Remove the stencil design from the freezer and leave it on its pan. Spread the batter over the tuile décor with a large offset spatula, making sure you have an even thickness across the pan. Place a second sheet pan under the first to help keep the bottom from browning.

Bake for about 12 minutes, rotating once after 6 minutes. The cake is done when the top springs back and is dry to the touch and just starting to brown on the top. If overcooked, the cake will become crunchy toward the edges or in shallow spots. Allow to cool.

COCONUT MERINGUE

30 g powdered sugar

30 g unsweetened shredded coconut

2 g (1 tsp) freshly ground black pepper

80 g egg whites

80 g granulated sugar

Preheat the oven to 350°F (175°C). Trace a 20-centimeter (8-in) cake ring twice onto a half sheet of parchment. Place the template on a half sheet pan with a silicone baking mat on top.

Sift the powdered sugar into a large bowl and add the coconut and pepper. Prepare a French meringue (see page 191) with the egg whites and granulated sugar, whisking to very stiff peak. Due to the high proportion of sugar to egg whites in this recipe you can whisk away with confidence, as there is little risk of overwhisking the meringue. Just make sure it is stiff. Fold the meringue into the coconut and sugar until combined.

Using a 1-centimeter (0.4-in) pastry tip, pipe the meringue onto the silicone mat in a spiral, starting in the center. Fill the template circles but leave a 1.25-centimeter (0.5-in) space around the edge.

Bake until the meringue is dry to the touch and just starting to brown, about 20 to 22 minutes. When cool, the meringue should be crisp on the outside and edges but still chewy on the inside.

STRAWBERRY MOUSSE

12 g powdered gelatin

60 g cold water

350 g strawberry puree

175 g powdered sugar

350 g heavy cream

In a medium, microwave-safe bowl, combine the gelatin with the cold water and stir well until dissolved. Let it sit for 5 minutes to bloom.

Place the puree in a medium saucepan. Sift the powdered sugar and whisk it into the puree. Heat the puree over medium heat until slightly warm, about 2 minutes.

In the bowl of the stand mixer fitted with the whisk attachment, whisk the cream to soft peak.

Melt the gelatin on low in the microwave. Swirl the bowl to stir the gelatin every 30 seconds, until it is completely melted. Slowly add one-third of the slightly warm puree to the gelatin while whisking constantly. Add the remaining puree and whisk to combine. Add half of the puree to the cream and fold with a whisk, followed by the second half. Use immediately (see Assembly, page 155).

STRAWBERRY MIRROR

5 g powdered gelatin

25 g cold water

75 g Soaking Syrup (page 198)

75 g strawberry puree

In a small bowl, combine the gelatin with the cold water and stir well until dissolved. Let it sit for 5 minutes to bloom.

In a small saucepan, heat the soaking syrup until hot. Add the gelatin and stir until melted. Slowly stir in the puree. Refrigerate.

ASSEMBLY

Sugar, for dusting

70 g strawberry jam

Shredded coconut, as desired

Strawberries, as desired

Lightly dust the joconde cake top with granulated sugar so it will not stick when unmolding. Cut around the edges to break the cake away from the sides of the pan. Place a piece of parchment over the cake and flip it upside down. Remove the silicone mat slowly, starting at one corner and pulling the mat not up, but almost parallel to the mat itself in the opposite direction. If the cake is sticking or breaking, place it in the freezer for 15 minutes and try again.

With the cake horizontal in front of you, trim the bottom so you have a clean, straight edge. Make a parallel cut 4.5 centimeters (1.75 in) above the edge. Then make another the same distance above that so you have 2 strips of cake of the same width. Trim the ends of the strips. Use a 20-centimeter (8-in) cake ring as a guide to cut a circle about 2.5 centimeters (1 in) smaller out of the remaining cake. Then line the ring with acetate and place it on a half sheet pan lined with parchment.

Place one strip of cake against the inside of the mold, design facing the ring. Line up the ends of the first and second strips of cake in the mold and roll the cake around the ring until they overlap. Cut the second strip, leaving about a 2.5-centimeter (1-in) overlap. Push the cake ends together until the cake is nice and snug all the way around, leaving no gap or overlap.

Prepare the mousse. Place a disk of the meringue in the bottom of the cake ring. Add one-third of the mousse and spread flat. Top the mousse with the cake circle and then add another third of the mousse. Spread the jam on the remaining meringue and place it on the mousse, jam side up. Use the remaining mousse to fill the ring. Level the top using a large offset spatula. Freeze overnight.

Heat the strawberry glaze just enough to melt it but not make it hot, stirring carefully as not to introduce any air bubbles. Pour it on the top of the frozen dessert, still in the cake ring, to hide the mousse. Refrigerate for 5 minutes to set the glaze. Slide the cake ring off the dessert and peel off the acetate. Decorate with shredded coconut and fresh strawberries.

PÉTANQUE

DIFFICULTY: 🍪 🍪 🍪

May the best man win.

Pétanque is a game of boules, similar to the Italian bocce, originating from the south of France. It is not uncommon to see teams of older men congregating in the local square for a friendly (but competitive!) game of pétanque after lunch or on weekends. The objective is to get your boules closest to the cochonnet ("piglet" in French) target ball to score points.

This is the most time-consuming dessert to make in the book, but it's also very delicious! If you are short on time, you can skip the pétanque court and the players. Double the hazelnut cake, cut it into two same-size rectangles and layer with the marmalade, "chocolate gravel" and praliné cream. Cover the sides with praliné cream and reserve some caramelized nuts from the praliné for décor.

Praliné is caramelized nuts ground to a paste. It's delicious. You can buy premade paste or make your own with this recipe. If you do not have blanched nuts, you can toast them first to remove the skins.

For this recipe, you will need a cake board or platter 16 x 30 centimeters (6.3 x 12 in) or larger to build the cake on.

YIELD: 8 servings

HAZELNUT CAKE

42 g powdered sugar

42 g hazelnut meal

36 g eggs

20 g egg yolks

35 g all-purpose flour

75 g egg whites

28 g granulated sugar

Preheat the oven to 350°F (180°C). Line a half sheet pan with a silicone baking mat.

In the bowl of a stand mixer fitted with the whisk attachment, whisk the powdered sugar, hazelnut meal, eggs and egg yolks until light and fluffy, about 5 minutes. Transfer the batter to a bigger bowl with a larger surface area on top. Sift the flour over the mixture and fold to incorporate.

Prepare a French meringue (see page 191) with the egg whites and granulated sugar, whisking to stiff peak. Fold half of the meringue into the hazelnut batter. Once combined, fold in the second half. Spread the mixture onto one-third of the half sheet pan. If your meringue was nice and stiff, the batter should not move after spreading. Bake until the top of the cake is dry and slightly golden, about 20 to 22 minutes.

PÉTANQUE COURT

250 g dark chocolate

Mark and cut out 2 templates from poster board or cardboard of similar thickness. An X-ACTO knife or razor blade works well for this. Make one 5 x 28 centimeters (2 x 11 in) and the other 12 x 28 centimeters (5 x 11 in).

Place a piece of parchment vertically on a flat surface. Temper the chocolate (see Techniques, page 190). Spread the chocolate in an evenly thick layer over the parchment, leaving a small boarder around the edges. Allow the chocolate to cool and start to solidify for a couple of minutes.

As soon as you can touch it without chocolate sticking to your finger, it's time to cut. Place the narrow template vertically on the chocolate to the far left. With a small knife, cut around all 4 sides of the template. Move the template to the right so the left side matches up with the cut edge. Cut around the template. Repeat a third time so you have 3 long rectangles. Cut the last rectangle exactly in half to yield 2 (5 x 14 centimeter [2 x 5.5 in]) shorter rectangles. Finally, cut a piece of chocolate the size of the larger template. Place a clean piece of parchment on top of the chocolate and weigh it down with something flat and heavy, such as a wood cutting board or large book. Allow the chocolate to solidify completely for 10 minutes.

Remove the board and top piece of parchment. Separate the pieces from the chocolate scraps and flip them over.

> **PARLOR TRICK!** Use a fine grade sandpaper to gently scratch the surface of the chocolate pieces for a more wood-like effect.

Take one of the longer pieces and place it horizontally on its edge against a sturdy cutting board or book with a straight right angle, presentation side, against the board. Line up the larger base piece on the counter and perpendicular to it. Gently reheat and temper the chocolate scraps. Make a small paper piping cone (see Techniques, page 190). Pipe the chocolate along the inside edges of the box to hold the 2 pieces together. Allow to set and then repeat with the other side. Allow to set and then turn the box by 90 degrees. Attach the shorter sides in the same manner. There will be some overhang of the end pieces.

After cutting the chocolate, separate the pieces from the scraps and turn them over. Pipe chocolate along the inside edges of the box so that it holds the shape.

ORANGE SYRUP

45 g Soaking Syrup (page 198)

35 g fresh orange juice

In a small bowl, combine syrup with the orange juice. Set aside.

HAZELNUT ALMOND PRALINÉ

220 g sugar

50 g water

115 g blanched hazelnuts

115 g blanched almonds

Place a silicone baking mat on a half sheet pan.

In a small saucepan, combine the sugar and water. Heat the sugar mixture until it reaches 240°F (116°C). Add the hazelnuts and almonds and stir with a wooden spoon to coat. Continue to cook over medium heat, stirring about every 5 seconds. The sugar will seize up and crystalize. Then, with time, the sugar will melt again and caramelize. As it starts to caramelize, stir constantly. Once the nuts are fragrant and coated in a golden brown caramel, remove from the heat and pour the nuts onto the silicone mat. Spread out into a single layer and allow to cool. Once cool, grind in a food processor to a paste, about 5 minutes.

PASTRY CREAM FOR PRALINÉ CREAM (RECIPE FOLLOWS)

350 g milk

75 g egg yolks

88 g sugar

28 g cornstarch

18 g unsalted butter, softened

In a medium, microwave-safe bowl, combine all the pastry cream ingredients. Blend with an immersion blender and then place the bowl in the microwave. Cook on high until the top and sides of the pastry cream are set and jiggle like Jell-O when you shake the bowl, 3 to 5 minutes. The center will still be a bit liquid and the sides almost curdled. With a clean immersion blender, blend the pastry cream to combine, scrape the sides of the bowl and continue to blend in the center and also just at the surface until smooth. If, after blending, the cream is still very runny and has not thickened, continue to cook and blend until you have the consistency of pudding. Cover the surface with plastic wrap and refrigerate.

PRALINÉ CREAM

500 g prepared pastry cream

250 g unsalted butter, softened

125 g hazelnut almond praliné

10 g (2 tsp) vanilla extract

Place the pastry cream in the bowl of the stand mixer fitted with the paddle attachment. Mix on high speed until smooth, about 30 seconds.

In a separate mixer bowl, beat the butter on high speed with the paddle attachment until very soft, about 4 minutes. Add the praliné and mix to combine. Add the pastry cream and switch out the paddle attachment for the whisk. Whisk on medium speed to combine, then increase the speed to high and whisk for 5 minutes. The mixture should be light and fluffy. Add the vanilla and whisk to combine.

CHOCOLATE "GRAVEL"

70 g dark chocolate

26 g unsalted butter

100 g hazelnut almond praliné

70 g pailleté feuilletine

In a small, microwave-safe bowl, combine the chocolate and butter and microwave on low, stirring often, just until melted. Stir in the praliné and the pailleté feuilletine. Use immediately (see Assembly, page 161).

NOTE: Pailleté feuilletine is essentially very thin, flaky dehydrated crepes. Its main purpose is to give texture. If you cannot find it, substitute crushed fortune cookies or corn flakes.

THE PLAYERS

1 recipe pâte à choux (page 172)

1 recipe craquelin (page 112)

20 g orange marmalade

200 g prepared praliné cream

Marzipan, as needed

Black food coloring, as needed

Dark chocolate, as needed

Preheat the oven to 350°F (175°C). Line a half sheet pan with a silicone baking mat.

Pipe 3 (4 centimeter [1.5 in]) cream puffs and 3 (3 centimeter [1.2 in]) puffs onto the mat. Cut pieces of craquelin to the same diameters and place on top of each of the puffs. Bake until set and light golden brown, about 25 minutes for the smaller ones. Pull the small puffs off the pan and bake the larger puffs an additional 5 minutes. Place on a wire rack to cool.

Using a 1-centimeter (0.4-in) open tip, pipe a small amount of marmalade into the bottom of each of the large cream puffs. With a slightly smaller tip, continue to fill the large puffs along with the smaller puffs with the praliné cream. Place the smaller puff on top of the larger. Using a very small star pastry tip, pipe the praliné cream in a ruffle around the area where the large and small puffs meet.

Mix a small amount of the remaining marzipan with the black food coloring. Roll tiny log-shape pieces and form them into 3 mustaches. Roll out the rest flat and cut out circles for the berets. Allow to dry out overnight. Attach them to the players with a small amount of melted chocolate.

PÉTANQUE BOULES AND COCHONNET

0.5 g (¼ tsp) silver luster dust

Drop of water

6 dark chocolate pearls (Crunchy Pearls by Valrhona or the Crispy Pearls by Callebaut)

1 piece acini di pepe pasta

Orange food coloring, as needed

Place the silver dust in a small bowl. Add the drop of water and mix together with a brush. Brush the chocolate pearls with the silver color. Color the pasta with the orange coloring. Allow all the pieces to dry.

ASSEMBLY

120 g orange marmalade

Place the chocolate pétanque court on a cake board or platter.

Unmold the hazelnut cake and cut into a piece 12 x 27 centimeters (4.7 x 10.5 in). Place the cake in the bottom of the chocolate mold. In a small saucepan, warm the orange syrup to a simmer. Using a pastry brush, generously soak the cake with the orange syrup, being careful not to touch and melt the chocolate.

Evenly spread 120 grams of marmalade over the cake to cover it completely.

Top with the remaining praliné cream and spread evenly to cover the marmalade. Refrigerate for 30 minutes to firm up the cream. Meanwhile prepare the chocolate "gravel" and allow it to cool to room temperature.

Remove the entremet from the refrigerator. Spread the chocolate "gravel" evenly over the praliné cream. Return to the refrigerator to set up.

Arrange the players, boules and cochonnet on the court.

CHAPTER FIVE

PETITS FOURS

Otherwise known as "little ovens," French petits fours are small, two- to three-bite-size pastries. Petits fours are perfect for afternoon tea, buffets, cocktail parties and more. When planning a party, we recommend making four or five petits fours per guest. Keep in mind the more variety of petits fours you offer, the more your guests will want to try one of everything!

LEMON POPPY SEED MACARONS

DIFFICULTY:

Foolproof recipe, just for you.

Possibly the most popular French pastry in modern times. Macarons need little introduction, but lots of instruction! You have just three ingredients (eggs, sugar, almonds), but time and time again, attempts to make them are far from stellar or completely unsuccessful. It's all about technique.

We added a touch of Americana with our bright, citrusy, lemon poppy seed version.
But change the color and flavor on a whim.

YIELD: 32 macarons

LEMON VANILLA BUTTERCREAM

250 g Vanilla Buttercream (page 194)

75 g fresh lemon juice

Bring the buttercream to room temperature. Place it in the bowl of a stand mixer fitted with the paddle attachment and beat it on high speed until very soft, about 4 minutes. Add the lemon juice, little by little, beating each addition smooth again before adding more. If the mixture does not come together and form an emulsion, pass a propane torch over the sides and bottom of the bowl just enough to warm the buttercream a tad but not enough melt it.

MACARONS

245 g powdered sugar

165 g almond meal, blanched

145 g egg whites

70 g granulated sugar

Yellow food coloring, as desired

5 g poppy seeds

Preheat the oven to 350°F (175°C). Line 2 half sheet pans with silicone baking mats and then place a second pan under each of them.

Place the powdered sugar and the almond meal in a food processor. Process for 30 seconds to get a more refined almond meal. Sift this mixture into a wide, large bowl and set aside. Prepare a French meringue (see page 191) with the egg whites and granulated sugar, whisking to stiff peak. Due to the high proportion of sugar to egg whites in this recipe, you can whisk away with confidence, as there is little risk of overwhisking the meringue. When your meringue is finished, add coloring until the desired shade is reached.

Add all the meringue to the almond mixture. Now we start what I call the "Fold, Smear, Smear" technique. Using a plastic bowl scraper, fold the almond meal through and over the meringue once. Then, use the bowl scraper to smear the meringue and almonds against the bowl twice. In addition to incorporating the meringue with the almonds, we are purposely deflating our meringue. Continue to fold once, then smear twice, until your batter just barely runs like very, very slow lava. I mean so slow you have to really stop and stare at it to see it move. This is the most crucial step in making macarons—the mixing. In French there is even a name for this step—le macaronage. Overmix and the macarons will be tough, hard and flat. Undermix and the macarons will have bumpy tops.

Place the macaron mixture in a piping bag fitted with a 1.25-centimeters (0.5-in) tip. Holding the tip 1.25 centimeters (0.5 in) above the baking mat, pipe straight down without moving the tip until you have a 3.5-centimeter (1.4-in) circle. Stop applying pressure to the bag and, with a quick circular flick of the wrist, pull the tip away from the batter. Be sure to leave at least 2.5 centimeters (1 in) in between the macarons.

After you have piped the entire pan, the macaron tops should have a slight bump on the top where you removed the piping tip. Lift up the top pan and lightly hit the bottom of it in multiple areas. By doing this, the batter should spread slightly and the bumps should go away. If they don't, tap the pan a few more times. If you finish piping the pan and the macrons have already spread and have smooth tops, you may have overmixed the batter a bit. Sprinkle the tops generously with poppy seeds. Bake for about 18 minutes. If you put a finger on one of the macaron tops and try to wiggle it slightly, it should not move. If it does, bake for another minute or so. Remove the bottom pans and allow the macarons to cool. Once cool, the macarons should have a firm top, soft center and the renowned crackled rim called the "foot."

PARLOR TRICK! Always double-pan macarons when baking, or use a heavy-duty steel pan as they do in France. If you don't, your macarons will have cracked tops.

sure your meringue is stiff.

Fold the almond meal through and over the meringue.

ear the mixture against the bowl.

And smear again. Repeat.

Stop folding when the batter flows so slowly you have to stare at it to see it move.

Before filling your piping bag, use your thumb to push part of the bag into the so nothing can leak out as you fill the bag.

Right after piping, the macarons should have small bumps on their tops. Tapping the bottom of the tray will eliminate them.

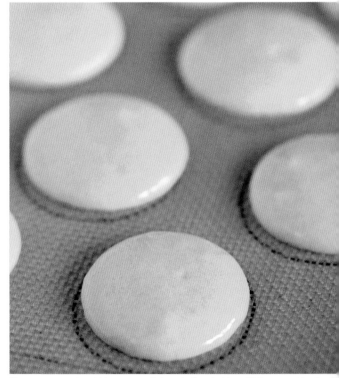

The macarons should have smooth tops before baking. (But no need to dry th out as stated in other recipes.)

ASSEMBLY

Remove the macarons from the baking mats by sliding a small offset spatula under their bottom. Make sure your buttercream is at room temperature and very soft. If it is not, using the paddle attachment of the stand mixer, beat it on high speed again. Using a 1-centimeter (0.5-in) open piping tip, pipe a small amount of buttercream in the center of a macaron half and sandwich it together with the other half, wiggling it in tiny circles to push the buttercream to the edges. Macarons should be eaten at room temperature and within 2 days. The best way to store macarons is to freeze them, pulling them out to thaw as desired.

MINIATURE BOURBON ÉCLAIRS

DIFFICULTY:

Soon to trounce the macaron?

The éclair has made a resurgence in Paris in recent years as it's given itself a makeover. The new éclair now is always covered with craquelin for a bit of crunch and comes in a rainbow of colors and flavors beyond the classic chocolate and coffee we once knew them for. With that said, fill them with whatever you want . . . the possibilities are endless.

YIELD: 30 mini éclairs

CRAQUELIN

68 g unsalted butter

80 g brown sugar

80 g all-purpose flour

Every good eclair must be topped with craquelin!

In the bowl of a stand mixer fitted with the paddle attachment, mix together the butter and brown sugar on medium speed until smooth, about 2 minutes. Add the flour and mix on low speed until sandy, about 1 minute. Pour onto a silicone baking mat and squeeze the mixture in your hands until it starts to stick together. Top it with a second silicone baking mat, smooth side down.

Roll the dough between the smooth sides of the mats into a rough 28-centimeter (11-in) square about the thickness of a credit card. Thinner is better, as the craquelin can weigh down the eclairs and restrict their rising. Peel back the top mat and replace it with a piece of parchment. Holding the 2 corners of the paper and the mat farthest from you, lift and flip the craquelin over so the parchment is on the bottom. Peel back the second silicone mat. If the mats are sticking to the craquelin, put them in the freezer for 10 minutes.

Using a ruler as a guide, cut a straight edge along the bottom of the craquelin. Move the ruler up 6 centimeters (2.5 in) and make a parallel cut. Continue until cutting rows until you reach the top edge of the craquelin. Then, cut individual pieces, 2.5 centimeters (1 in) wide, from the rows, leaving them in place on the parchment. Any scraps can be rerolled, if needed. Freeze the craquelin.

PÂTE À CHOUX

85 g milk

85 g water

4 g salt

8 g sugar

85 g unsalted butter

95 g bread flour, sifted

170 g eggs

The pâte à choux is now ready for the eggs.

1- Too many eggs.
2- Not enough eggs.
3- Just right!

One of the core recipes of French pastry. The mixing and baking can be tricky at first. Be sure to follow the directions and these tips:

1. Be careful not to let the mixture boil before the butter has melted, or else some of your liquid may evaporate while waiting for the butter to melt. This changes the recipe.

2. The amount of eggs used will vary, depending how dry the mixture is. You may not need them all or you may need more.

3. Do not substitute other flours for bread flour. The extra gluten in bread flour has the needed strength to capture the steam released during cooking, leaving the void that will be filled with cream.

Preheat the oven to 350°F (175°C). Line 2 half sheet pans with silicone baking mats. In a medium saucepan, combine the milk, water, salt, sugar and butter. Warm the mixture over medium heat, stirring occasionally, until the butter is melted. Then, bring the mixture to a boil. Remove the pan from the heat, add all the flour at once and stir with a wooden spoon. Return the pan to the stove and continue to stir until all the liquid is absorbed and the mixture comes together. Once you see a film of dough on the bottom of the pan and the mixture starts to pull away from the sides and roll toward the middle, about 10 seconds, remove it from the heat. Transfer the mixture to the bowl of the stand mixer fitted with the paddle attachment. Mix on low speed for 1 minute to cool slightly.

Lightly mix the eggs to break up the yolks. Add about a fifth of the eggs to the warm batter and mix on medium speed until they are completely absorbed, about 30 seconds. Add another fifth and allow to incorporate. The eggs may slosh around a bit in the bowl, but slowly they will become absorbed. Continue adding eggs, little by little, until the batter starts to look glossy and to loosen up, scraping the bottom of the bowl often.

Before all the eggs are added, test the batter by running your finger through it to create a trough. If the tough stays stiff, add more eggs. If the trough slowly moves back inward, but does not close completely, stop. This step is crucial. Adding too many eggs or not enough eggs will affect its ability to rise in the oven. Err on the side of less egg, as with too much egg your choux may end up flat.

Place the pâte à choux in a piping bag fitted with a 1-centimeter (0.5-in) pastry tip. Pipe the dough in 6-centimeter (2.5-in) straight lines on a silicone baking mat. At the end of the éclair, stop applying pressure to the bag and flick your wrist slightly down and then up to release the dough from the tip. Leave a 5-centimeter (2-in) space between each éclair for rising space. Gently place a piece of craquelin on the top of each one.

Place the éclairs in the oven, spacing the pans evenly. Bake until the craquelin and the éclair bottoms are light golden brown, about 30 minutes. Do not open the oven door the first 20 minutes. When they are done, immediately remove the éclairs from the pans and place on a wire rack to cool.

BOURBON PASTRY CREAM

500 g milk

100 g egg yolks

125 g sugar

40 g cornstarch

25 g unsalted butter

28 g bourbon

In a microwave-safe bowl, combine all the pastry cream ingredients, except the bourbon. Blend them with an immersion blender and then place the bowl in the microwave. Cook on high until the top and sides of the pastry cream are set and jiggle like Jell-O when you shake the bowl, 5 to 7 minutes. The center will still be a bit liquid and the sides almost curdled. With a clean immersion blender, mix the pastry cream to combine, scrape the sides of the bowl and continue to blend in the center and also just at the surface until smooth. If, after blending, the cream is still very runny and has not thickened, continue to cook and blend until you have the consistency of pudding. Cover the surface with plastic wrap and refrigerate.

Transfer the cold pastry cream to the bowl of the stand mixer fitted with the paddle attachment. Mix on high speed until smooth, about 30 seconds. Stir in the bourbon.

CHERRY PUREE

175 g Amarena cherries, well strained

Puree the cherries in a food processor.

CHOCOLATE DÉCOR

400 g dark chocolate

Trace the template (page 198) 30 times onto the smooth side of a chocolate transfer (see Equipment and Ingredient Sources, page 199) sheet and cut them out. Temper the dark chocolate in the microwave (see Techniques, page 190). Spread the chocolate, using a small offset spatula, onto the tacky side of the transfer sheet. Place into paper towel rolls cut in half to curve the sides while the chocolate sets. Work quickly. You may need to rewarm the chocolate just a tiny bit in the microwave, but don't overheat it or it will be out of temper. After about 15 minutes, remove the plastic.

ASSEMBLY

Place the pastry cream in a piping bag tightly fitted with a small round pastry tip. Pierce the bottom of the éclair in the center and fill while angling the tip toward each end. Pipe a thin line of pureed cherries along the top. Attach the chocolate décor to the cherries. Once filled, éclairs should be eaten within 24 hours.

BLUE CHEESE TRUFFLES

DIFFICULTY:

Yes, we did just go there.

Once again, we have the winning combination of salty and sweet! Super easy to make and they don't require you to temper the chocolate. When choosing a blue cheese go with Roquefort for more intensity and saltiness or Bleu d'Auvergne for a milder, creamy flavor.

YIELD: 30 truffles

CARAMEL GANACHE

60 g milk chocolate

60 g dark chocolate

150 g heavy cream

30 g glucose or corn syrup

165 g sugar

58 g blue cheese

Pan release spray

Place the chocolates in a medium bowl with a strainer over it and set aside. In a small saucepan, bring the cream to a simmer. Remove it from the heat and set aside.

In a large saucepan, melt the glucose over medium heat, about 30 seconds. Add half of the sugar and stir. Allow the sugar to melt a bit, about 30 seconds, and stir again. Add the rest of the sugar and stir. Allow to melt a bit and stir again.

Continue to cook, now stirring constantly, to caramelize the sugar. Right when the mixture turns a deep caramel color, remove the pan from the heat and slowly add the hot cream. Stir well to combine and then strain into the chocolate. Let the mixture sit for 1 minute to melt the chocolate and then whisk it until smooth. Add the blue cheese and let it sit for another minute. Whisk to combine (a few small unmelted pieces of cheese is okay) and place in the refrigerator.

Once the ganache has set up, remove it from the refrigerator. Scoop portions of ganache, about 10 grams each, and place them on a half sheet lined with parchment and sprayed with pan release. After you have portioned all the ganache, roll the ganache into loose balls (we are not looking for perfect spheres). If they are too sticky to roll, place them in the refrigerator for 10 minutes. After rolling, place the ganache balls in the freezer.

ASSEMBLY

60 g dark alkalized cocoa powder

10 g blue luster dust

350 g dark chocolate

Mix the cocoa powder with the luster dust in a wide, shallow bowl. Melt the chocolate in the microwave on low, stirring often.

Remove the ganache balls from the freezer. Toss one ball into the melted chocolate and turn it around with a fork to cover. Lift the ganache out of the chocolate with the fork and tap it on the side of the bowl to remove any excess chocolate. Flip the fork over to drop the ganache into the cocoa mixture. Make sure the spot where the fork was touching the ganache is covered with chocolate. Gently push the truffle with your finger a few times to create the characteristic wrinkles of a real mushroom truffle. Continue with a few more truffles. Once the chocolate has set, you can remove the truffles from the cocoa and set them on a clean sheet pan.

After all the truffles are coated, chill them in the refrigerator to be sure the chocolate has hardened. Place the truffles in a strainer and shake to remove any excess cocoa powder. Extra cocoa powder can be sifted and reused.

PARLOR TRICK! Since we are freezing the ganache, we do not need to temper our enrobing chocolate. The cold centers will shock the chocolate and make it set up quickly.

CRÈME BRÛLÉE COOKIES

DIFFICULTY:

Always a crowd-pleaser.

Class up your crème brûlée with a bit of Grand Marnier orange liqueur. The tart dough base not only adds crunch, but acts as a carrier for the cream. So easy to make and you can take these to a party and not worry about getting your crème brûlée ramekins back at the end of the night.

For this recipe, you will need two 4-centimeter (1.5-in) silicone demisphere molds with fifteen cavities per mold.

YIELD: 30 cookies

SWEET TART DOUGH

50 g egg yolks

2.5 g (½ tsp) vanilla extract

155 g all-purpose flour, plus more for rolling and baking

Pinch of salt

70 g powdered sugar

120 g unsalted butter, cold

In a small bowl, whisk together the egg yolks and vanilla and set aside. Sift the flour, salt and sugar into the bowl of a stand mixer fitted with the paddle attachment and combine on low speed. Cut the butter into 1-centimeter (0.5-in) cubes and add it to the flour mixture. Continue to mix on low speed until the mixture resembles coarse sand, about 5 minutes. Do not overmix. If the mixture starts to stick together, it will not absorb the eggs and it will be very sticky and hard to roll. Add the egg yolks and vanilla and mix just until incorporated and you have a homogenous dough, about 30 seconds. Form the dough into a flattened circle and wrap it in plastic wrap. Refrigerate for 1 hour, minimum.

Preheat the oven to 350°F (175°C). Line a half sheet pan with a silicone baking mat.

Roll out the pâte sucrée 0.5 centimeters (0.2 in) thick. Using a 4.5-centimeter (1.75-in) pastry cutter, cut 30 circles from the dough and place them on the half sheet. Refrigerate the dough for 15 minutes to prevent spreading. Bake the circles just until the edges are golden brown, 10 to 12 minutes.

CRÈME BRÛLÉE

85 g egg yolks

60 g sugar, plus more for sprinkling

350 g heavy cream

10 g Grand Marnier

2.5 g (½ tsp) vanilla extract

Preheat the oven to 300°F (150°C). Place 2 (4 centimeter [1.5 in]) silicone demisphere molds with 15 cavities per mold on a half sheet pan.

In a small bowl, combine all the crème brûlée ingredients and blend them with an immersion blender. Fill the molds with the crème brûlée. Pass the flame of a propane torch over the surface of the cavities to pop any bubbles. Place the half sheet pan in the oven, but before closing the door, pour 1 centimeter (0.5 in) of warm tap water into the pan around the molds. Close the oven door and bake until the crème brûlée is set, about 25 to 30 minutes. When you lightly shake the pan, the crème brûlée should not move in the center. Allow to cool to room temperature, pour the water out of the pan and then place it in the freezer. Freeze for at least 6 hours.

ASSEMBLY

Gold leaf, as needed

Unmold the frozen crème brûlée and place a dome on each of the tart dough bases. Sprinkle a tiny amount of sugar on top of the crème brûlée. Caramelize the sugar with a propane torch, using the lowest setting. Decorate with gold leaf. Allow to thaw completely before serving, about 30 minutes in the refrigerator.

RASPBERRY ALMOND TEA CAKES

DIFFICULTY:

Cute as a button. But tastier.

These little almond cakes burst with flavor. That's why they work so well as petits fours. Serve them at room temperature, but make sure you try one fresh out of the oven. It will melt in your mouth!

For this recipe, you will need two 4-centimeter (1.5-in) silicone demisphere molds with fifteen cavities per mold.

YIELD: About 30 (3.8 centimeter [1.5 in]) petits fours

ALMOND CAKE BATTER

Pan release spray

50 g frozen raspberries

32 g pastry flour

320 g almond paste

70 g eggs

20 g egg yolks

50 g unsalted butter, melted

85 g (30 berries) fresh raspberries

Powdered sugar, as needed

Preheat the oven to 350°F (175°C). Place 2 (4 centimeter [1.5 in]) silicone demishpere molds with 15 cavities per mold on a half sheet pan and spray them with pan release.

Place the frozen raspberries in a food processor. Pulse the food processor briefly to break them up into small segments. Do this quickly and return them to the freezer.

Sift the flour and set aside. Place the almond paste in the bowl of a stand mixer fitted with the paddle attachment. Start mixing on medium speed. In a small bowl, combine the eggs and egg yolks and then slowly add them to the almond paste in 3 parts, making sure the last part is incorporated before adding the next. Scrape down the sides of the bowl as needed. Add the flour and mix just until combined, about 30 seconds. Add the melted butter and mix just until combined, about 10 seconds. Fold in the frozen raspberry pieces (make sure they are fully frozen).

Using a small offset spatula, spread the batter into the mold cavities, making sure the batter gets smeared on the bottom well so there are no air bubbles. Sink a fresh raspberry into each cavity and smooth the batter over it to fill the mold. If the raspberries are too large, you can break them into pieces that fit in the cavity.

Place a second half sheet pan under the first to prevent browning on what will be the cake tops when inverted. Bake until the batter is dry to the touch, has puffed slightly and the cakes have just started to brown around the edges, 18 to 20 minutes. Let the mold cool for a few minutes. Then, quickly flip the mold over onto a sheet pan and slowly roll the mold off the cakes, pinching the top of the cavities slightly if the cakes are sticking. Cool completely and then dust with powdered sugar.

BAKER'S DOZEN

DIFFICULTY: 🍪

Twelve for the party, one for the pastry chef.

For this recipe, you will need an egg decapitator and a 4-centimeter (1.5-in) silicone demisphere
mold with fifteen cavities per mold.

YIELD: One dozen + one "egg"

MANGO YOLKS

2 g (scant ½ tsp) powdered gelatin

10 g cold water

160 g mango puree

35 g sugar

In a small bowl, combine the gelatin with the cold water and stir well until dissolved. Let it sit for 5 minutes to bloom.

In a small saucepan, combine the puree and sugar and heat just until warm and the sugar is dissolved. Add the solid gelatin mass to the puree and stir until the gelatin is melted, then pour the mixture into 13 cavities of the demisphere mold. Freeze overnight.

COCONUT CREAM

425 g coconut puree

115 g milk

2 kaffir lime leaves

50 g eggs

30 g egg yolks (see Assembly)

18 g cornstarch

115 g sugar

In a medium saucepan, bring the puree and milk to a boil. Remove from the heat and add the lime leaves. Cover and let sit for 15 minutes. Remove the lime leaves and discard them.

In a medium bowl, combine the eggs, egg yolks from your decapitated eggs, cornstarch and sugar and whisk until pale. Slowly whisk the liquid into the egg mixture. Strain into a clean saucepan.

Over medium heat, whisk continually until the mixture starts to thicken. Pull off the heat and keep whisking while the mixture continues to thicken from the residual heat. Return the pan to the heat, still whisking, until the mixture boils, about 1 to 2 minutes, being careful not to burn the bottom. Remove from the heat and stir until it melts. Pour the cream into a bowl and place plastic wrap directly on top of the cream to prevent a skin from forming. Refrigerate immediately.

If you can get your hands on Thai kaffir lime leaves, include them. They are usually sold frozen in Asian grocery stores. It is okay to leave them out, but they give a nice aromatic dimension to the cream.

NOTE: I strongly recommend seeking out frozen coconut puree by Boiron, Perfect Puree or Ravifruit. The flavor is just so much brighter than the coconut milk you find in a can. Once you try it you'll be hooked. Use any leftover to make sorbet or a nice curry. If frozen puree is not available, canned coconut milk will work. (But get the frozen stuff!)

ASSEMBLY

13 large eggs

Using an egg decapitator and following the manufacturer's directions, decapitate the 13 eggs (save the whites for another use and use the yolks in the coconut cream). Wash the shells in soapy water. Rinse well and allow to dry. The egg whites will leave a thin skin in the shells. If it pulls away from the side, you can pull it out, but it is not necessary.

Place the shells in an egg carton and one in an egg cup. Pipe about 45 grams of the coconut cream into each shell. Unmold the frozen "yolks" and and place them on a piece of parchment paper. Cut off the edges, using a 3-centimeter (1.2-in) circle pastry cutter, so you can fit the yolk into the eggshell. Place the "yolks" into the eggshells with the help of a small offset spatula.

EARL GREY NAPOLEONS

DIFFICULTY:

It's three p.m. Tea time!

These stacked cookies are both crunchy and creamy in the same bite and more bittersweet
from the chocolate and cocoa than sweet. Search out a high-quality, loose-leaf tea,
ideally from a tea shop.

YIELD: 30 petits fours

CHOCOLATE ALMOND DOUGH

68 g powdered sugar

18 g cocoa powder

150 g all-purpose flour, plus more for
rolling and baking

22 g almond meal

2.5 g (½ tsp) salt

90 g unsalted butter, cold

50 g eggs

Sift the sugar, cocoa and flour into the bowl of a stand mixer fitted with the paddle
attachment. Add the almond meal and salt. Stir to combine. Cut the butter into
1-centimeter (0.5-in) cubes and add it to the bowl. Mix on low speed until the mixture
resembles coarse sand, about 5 minutes. Add the eggs and mix just until the dough
starts to stick together, about 2 minutes. Do not overmix. Form the dough into a
flattened circle and wrap it in plastic wrap. Refrigerate for 1 hour, minimum.

Preheat the oven to 350°F (175°C). Line 2 half sheet pans with silicone baking mats.

Roll the dough into a rough square about 28 centimeters (11 in) in size. The dough
should be 0.5 centimeters (0.2 in) thick. Using a ruler as a guide, cut a straight edge
along the bottom of the dough. Move the ruler up 5 centimeters (2 in) and make a
parallel cut. Continue cutting rows until you have 5 rows total. Then, cut individual
pieces 2 centimeters (0.75 in) wide from the rows, 12 per row, for a total of 60.

Using a small offset spatula, transfer the pieces to the baking mats. Any scraps can be
rerolled, if needed. Refrigerate the dough for 15 minutes to prevent spreading. Bake the
pieces just until they look firm and are dry to the touch, about 8 to 10 minutes.

EARL GREY WHIPPED GANACHE

125 g heavy cream, plus 250 g, cold

7 g Earl Grey tea, loose leaf

100 g dark chocolate

In a small saucepan, bring the 125 grams of cream to a simmer. Remove from the heat and add the tea. Cover and infuse for 5 minutes, or as directed by the producer. Strain the cream and discard the tea. In a medium microwave-safe bowl, melt the chocolate in the microwave on low, stirring often. Pour one-third of the hot cream into the chocolate. Whisk vigorously in the center of the bowl. Once the center starts to emulsify and look glossy, start whisking in larger and larger circles until all the chocolate is incorporated. Add the next third of the cream and repeat the same procedure, followed by the last third of cream. The ganache should be glossy and smooth. Whisk in the cold cream. Refrigerate for 4 or more hours.

Remove the cream from the refrigerator. Transfer to the bowl of the stand mixer fitted with the whisk attachment and whisk on high speed just until stiff peak, about 15 seconds. Refrigerate until ready to use.

ASSEMBLY

25 g candied orange rind

20 g cocoa powder

2 g (1 tsp) gold dust

Gold leaf, as needed

Finely chop the orange rind. Combine the cocoa powder and the gold dust. Using a small rose petal piping tip, pipe the ganache onto 30 of the chocolate cookies, keeping the piping tip upright and using a back and forth motion. Place a small amount of the candied orange rind on top of the ganache. Top with a second cookie and pipe the ganache in the same way on those. Lightly sprinkle the napoleons with the décor powder and top with a piece of gold leaf.

PARLOR TRICK! Before piping the ganache, place the chocolate cookies on a dish towel to prevent them from sliding around while being covered.

CHOCOLATE NOUGATINE

DIFFICULTY:

My version of "cookies."

This is a crunchy treat that balances the sweetness of the caramel with dark chocolate and bitter cocoa nibs. While this recipe has few ingredients, it requires a higher degree of technique. Be sure not to overcook your caramel. If it hardens before you get it cut, just break off pieces with your hands. Why not?

YIELD: 30 pieces

ALMOND NOUGATINE

Pan release spray

115 g sliced blanched almonds

215 g sugar

300 g dark chocolate

10 g cocoa nibs

Preheat the oven to 300°F (150°C). Spray both a piece of parchment and the smooth side of a silicone baking mat with pan release. Place the sprayed parchment on a cutting board.

Place the almonds on a half sheet pan and toast in the oven just until lightly golden, about 15 minutes. You will want to use these while still warm.

Make a dry caramel by placing one-fourth of the sugar in a saucepan on medium heat. When you see the edges start to melt, stir briefly with a wooden spoon and allow the edges to melt again. Stir again and repeat until all the sugar is melted but not fully caramelized. Add the rest of the sugar, one-fourth at a time, and follow the same procedure (see Techniques, page 190). If you get lumps in the sugar, pull it off the heat and stir until they melt before continuing. Cook the sugar until golden caramel in color, testing it by smearing a small amount on a white piece of parchment paper. Add the warm almonds all at once and stir to coat completely.

Pour the almonds onto the parchment paper. Place the silicone baking mat, smooth side down, on top of the almonds and press on it to flatten the mass. Using a rolling pin, roll the nougatine to a thickness of about 0.5 centimeter (0.2 in). Try to lift up one edge of the silicone mat. If it sticks, wait 10 seconds and try again. As soon as the mat no longer sticks, roll it back a few centimeters, keeping the rest of the nougatine covered and thus warm. Cut 4-centimeter (1.5-in) circles quickly with a pastry cutter. When all the exposed nougatine is cut, roll the silicone mat back a few centimeters more. Continue until all the nougatine is cut. Once completely cool, remove the circles. Temper the chocolate in the microwave (see Techniques, page 190). Dip two-thirds of each circle in the chocolate and place them on the rough side of a silicone baking mat. Top with cocoa nibs. Store at room temperature and in an airtight container.

TECHNIQUES

MISE EN PLACE

Literally, "putting in place," mise en place is the act of having all your ingredients and equipment measured and at your disposal before starting to execute a recipe. I cannot stress enough the importance of mise en place when in the pastry kitchen.

USING A PIPING BAG

Using a piping bag is a simple technique, but if not done correctly, it can leave you with a big mess and unflattering results. Follow these easy steps:

1. Select the right-size bag. For ease of handling, you will want to fill up the pastry bag only two-thirds full. Use larger bags for filling up molds and smaller bags for detailed decorations.

2. Insert your piping tip inside the bag. Pull it down tight at the bottom until it is firmly stuck it the bag.

3. Use your thumb to push the part of the bag just above the tip into the tip, so nothing can leak out while you fill the bag.

4. Hold the bag in the middle and roll the top edge down over itself, like you're rolling up your sleeve.

5. Fill the bag two-thirds full, scraping the mixture off your spatula on the inside of the fold. You can do this while holding the bag or you can place the bag in a tall plastic container with the folded part over the container's edge, to balance it while you fill. See photo below.

6. Unfold the top of the bag and twist it so the end is closed.

7. When piping, apply pressure with only your dominate hand around the end of the bag. Use your other hand to lift up the tip and guide it in the right direction. Never squeeze the bag with both hands.

8. Always keep your piping tip in the air, letting the mixture fall into place. Never touch the dessert or drag your tip through it.

MAKING A PAPER CONE

1. Cut a triangle from a piece of parchment. Hold the straight longest edge up with a corner pointing down.

2. Curve the two side corners toward you and cross them, like they are giving someone a hug.

3. Keep wrapping them around themselves until they are all the way to the back and all three corners meet at a point on the bottom. Fold the point toward the inside of the cone, to secure it.

4. Fill the cone only one-third full. Once full, fold the top two corners toward the center at a diagonal, then fold the top open end down two times to close it. Snip off the end of the tip to pipe.

Tempering gelatin

INGREDIENT TEMPERING

Many recipes in this book will require you to temper one ingredient with another. With this technique you are bringing two ingredients to the same temperature very slowly so as not to have an adverse effect on one or the other. A perfect example would be combining hot milk and egg yolks. If you simply dumped all the eggs into the hot milk or vice versa, you could accidentally cook the eggs instead of incorporating them. By pouring the milk slowly into the egg yolks while stirring, the eggs will slowly warm to the same temperature as the milk and be perfectly incorporated. Another example is incorporating melted gelatin. The liquid to be combined with the melted gelatin should be slowly poured into the gelatin while stirring constantly, or else the gelatin may set up before the liquid is fully incorporated.

The same application applies to cold ingredients. When adding cold whipped cream to melted chocolate, you must do it little by little, or else the chocolate will get too cold and harden up into chips before it can be incorporated with the cream.

MERINGUES

Meringue recipes will tell you to whisk your meringue to either soft or stiff peaks. A meringue at soft peak is mixed for a shorter period of time. Finished, it will curve over slightly when you pull some out and hold it atop your finger. The French call this stage "bec d'oiseaux" as it resembles a bird's beak. A meringue at stiff peak will stand straight up in a peak on your finger. Meringue should be used immediately after it is made for best results. After time it becomes crumbly versus supple, so it's harder to fold into a mousse or batter nicely and won't hold its shape as well when piped.

There are three main types of meringues, each with properties that make it suitable for certain applications but not necessarily for others.

Top: Stiff peaks
Bottom: Soft peaks or as the French say, "bec d'oiseaux"

French Meringue

French meringues are used to lighten and give volume to cakes and batters that will be baked. It can also be baked on its own to create crunchy meringue pieces.

Basic Procedure: Using a stand mixer, whisk egg whites on high speed until foamy. Add half of the required sugar and continue to whisk. When the eggs are starting to take on volume and the color turns white, add the remaining sugar. Continue to whisk until the desired consistency is reached. For recipes with very small amounts of sugar, it is fine to add it all at the first addition. It is recommended to turn the mixer off for a second when adding the sugar, so it doesn't stick to the side of the bowl.

How much sugar is in a French meringue will determine its strength. Each large egg white can hold up to 50 grams of sugar. When the recipe contains a high proportion of sugar to whites, the meringue will become stiff and glossy and there is little chance that you will overwhisk it. This type of meringue is great for piping on its own. However, if the proportion of sugar to whites is low,

Adding sugar syrup to egg whites for Italian meringue.

Whipped cream at stiff peaks (left) and soft peaks (right).

the meringue will not be as strong. When folding this type of meringue into a batter, you must be very gentle, so it does not lose its volume. It is imperative that you keep a close eye on a meringue with little to no sugar as it finishes in the mixer. If you overmix it, the meringue will become crumbly and will not incorporate well into the rest of your recipe.

Italian Meringue

In an Italian meringue, the egg whites are cooked by pouring hot sugar syrup into them. It is very strong and durable. Since the whites are cooked by the sugar syrup, it can be used in mousses. It can also be baked in the oven on its own or piped and caramelized with a torch, as is often done on lemon tarts. Although this procedure requires a bit of skill, after some practice you'll prepare Italian meringue with ease.

Basic Procedure: In a saucepan, cook the sugar and water together on the stovetop. After you start cooking the sugar, place the egg whites in the bowl of a stand mixer fitted with the whisk attachment. When the sugar reaches 221°F (105°C) start whisking the egg whites on high speed. The goal is to bring the egg whites just to stiff peaks at the same time the sugar syrup reaches 245 to 250°F (118 to 121°C). When the syrup is in the correct range and the egg whites are at stiff peak, turn the mixer speed to low. Slowly pour the syrup down the side of the bowl and into the meringue, being careful not to pour it on the whisk. Once all the syrup is in, continue to whisk the mixture on low speed until cool.

Swiss Meringue

This is another form of meringue where the egg whites are cooked on the stovetop. It is stronger than a French meringue but doesn't have quite the strength of an Italian meringue. We do not use Swiss meringue in this book, but this is a brief introduction.

Basic Procedure: In the bowl of a stand mixer set over a bain-marie, whisk together the sugar and egg whites. When the mixture reaches 122°F (50°C), remove it from the heat, place the bowl on the stand mixer, and continue to whisk until cool.

WHISKING CREAM

Whipped cream is easy to make as long as you know when to stop the whipping. If you are making a sweetened whipped cream (crème chantilly in French) that you will pipe for a decoration, whisk your cream to stiff peaks. However, if your cream will be incorporated into a mousse, stop whisking when you reach a very soft peak, if even that, so the cream resembles more of a thick potato soup. It is very easy to overmix cream if you are not paying attention toward the end. If you overwhisk your cream by just a little bit, you can usually stir (not whisk) in a bit of liquid cream to loosen it up. It is often said to make whipped cream you must make sure the cream is very, very cold and to place your mixer bowl in the freezer ahead of time. Really not necessary. Really.

CARAMEL

Caramel comes in many forms—hard like glass, soft like fudge, and in varying degrees of liquid stages. Caramel is made by cooking sugar until it melts and changes color and flavor. If you let that sugar cool, it will become hard like glass. If, while the caramel is still hot, you add liquid (usually cream), the caramel will be soft or fluid, depending on how much liquid is added. Butter can also be added at this stage, for flavor.

It is recommended to use pure cane sugar when making caramel, as beet sugar tends to burn quickly. Copper pans retain heat well and are great for making caramels, if you can afford one. If you will be adding liquid to your caramel, choose to use a deep pot, as the liquid will bubble up when first added. Make sure your liquid is hot, so it will incorporate. Otherwise, the caramel will seize up. If this happens, return it to the stove and cook over low heat until it dissolves. Always have a container of ice water next to you when working with caramel. If some caramel gets on your hand, immerse it in the water immediately.

When making caramel, it is important to watch the color. Always test the color of the caramel on a white surface, such as a piece of parchment paper, as it can be hard to determine the color in a pan, especially a copper one. A caramel that is too light will taste sweet without complexity. A caramel cooked too dark will taste overly bitter or even burnt. Just like Goldilocks—you want it just right!

Some caramel recipes tell you to add water to your sugar in the beginning. Although this may help prevent burning, it takes a lot longer to caramelize because you first must evaporate all the water before the sugar will caramelize.

Basic Procedure: Place one-fourth of your sugar in a saucepan over medium heat. When you see the edges start to melt, stir briefly with a wooden spoon and allow the edges to melt again. Stir again and repeat until all the sugar is melted. It will have a light, opaque caramel color. Add the rest of the sugar, one-fourth at a time, and follow the same procedure. If your sugar starts to clump up or take on a lot of color before it is completely melted, continue to stir it off the heat, to slow down the cooking. If making a hard-crack caramel, cook the sugar until caramel in color and opaque. Continue stirring off the stove until the desired color is reached and the caramel looks transparent instead of opaque. You can always take it back to the stove if more heat is needed to reach the desired results. If the caramel is cooking too fast, you can slow or stop the cooking by removing the pan from the heat, placing the bottom of the pan on a wet towel, and stirring the mixture. For caramels involving cream, right when the correct color is reached, add the hot cream little by little and bat the rising foam back and forth with your spoon until it subsides. Then add more cream.

EMULSIONS

Most people think of mayonnaise or salad dressing when emulsions come to mind, but they happen very often in the pastry kitchen as well. Prime examples are ganache and flavored buttercreams. An emulsion is the coming together of a fat and a water-based substance, two things that normally don't mix well, to create a smooth, homogenous mixture. Temperature and agitation play a key role.

CHOCOLATE GANACHE

Care must be taken when making a ganache, to prevent it from separating. There must be a balance of fat (coming from chocolate, cream and butter) with any liquid (coming from cream, milk or flavorings). Usually when a ganache splits, it is because it is agitated while too cold or it simply contains too much fat. When adding cream to melted chocolate, do it in two or three stages, creating a satiny, smooth mixture while whisking briskly at each stage before adding more cream. Once your ganache is made, it is recommended to use it right away, as it can be difficult to reheat without separating.

Be sure to test the color of the caramel (top left). Add the rest of the sugar (top right). Cook until the desired color is reached (bottom left), and then add the cream (bottom right).

To create an emulsion of water based puree and butter cream, warm it gently with a torch while mixing.

Once set, it should jiggle like Jell-O (above). Mix again so that it reaches the right consistency (below).

BUTTERCREAM

Buttercream is often flavored with water-based fruit purees or alcohols. When flavoring unsalted buttercream, first bring your ingredients to room temperature. Place the buttercream in the bowl of a stand mixer fitted with the paddle attachment and beat it on medium-high speed. Wave a propane torch under the bottom of the bowl to soften, but not melt, the buttercream. When you touch the bowl, it should be neither hot nor cold. Once the buttercream is at room temperature and smooth, you can add your flavoring, little by little, letting each addition fully incorporate before adding more. If your flavoring is cold and you see the buttercream stiffen up, you can take the torch to the bottom of the bowl again.

MICROWAVE COOKING

The microwave can cook, steam and heat at a variety of heat levels. Because it does not involve direct bottom heat, you can use it to make pastry cream and lemon curd without stirring and without the risk of burning. It's magical! Simply place all your ingredients in a bowl, blend with an immersion blender and cook. Then immersion blend again. (Make sure you wash the immersion blender between mixing the raw cream and the finished cream.) The microwave is also the easiest way to temper small amounts of chocolate. You can use glass, plastic or stainless-steel bowls in the microwave. For stainless-steel bowls, make sure they do not touch the sides of the microwave.

Pastry Cream Basic Procedure: Place all the ingredients in a microwave-safe container. Blend with an immersion blender and then place in the microwave and cook on high power until the pastry cream is set and jiggles like Jell-O. Mix with the immersion blender once again, scraping down the container and blending again. If after blending, the cream is still very runny and has not thickened, continue to cook and blend until you have the consistency of pudding. Cover the surface with plastic wrap and refrigerate.

Lemon Curd Basic Procedure: Place all the ingredients in a microwave-safe container. Blend with an immersion blender and then place in the microwave and cook on high power until the mixture coats the back of a spoon. Check the curd after 2 minutes and every 30 seconds after. Every time you check, first blend with an immersion blender, as the mixture will not look smooth (but it's fine; trust me!). When you draw your finger through the curd while holding the spoon vertically (its edge facing up) the curds should not move.

ROLLING & BAKING TARTS

Always make sure you roll tart dough in a cool ambient temperature with the dough chilled. If it is too warm, the dough will stick to the rolling surface. Also, use plenty of flour on the surface, but not so much as to change the recipe! When dusting your rolling surface with flour, pretend you are skipping stones to scatter the flour evenly in a fine dust over the rolling surface versus sprinkling it in small piles. When rolling the dough, always start from the center of the mass and roll away from it. Roll toward the top. Roll toward the bottom. Then turn 90 degrees and repeat. With every turn, lightly dust the rolling surface as needed so the dough does not stick. Roll the dough to a thickness of 0.5 centimeter (0.2 in).

To line a tart mold or ring of any size, roll the dough about 4 centimeters (1.5 in) larger in size than the mold. It is recommended to spray molds with pan release and to flour gently to prevent sticking. Place the dough over the mold and gently sink it down into the corners. If using a ring, place it first on a piece of parchment that can be lifted onto a half sheet pan. Then, using a paring knife or your finger, cut the excess dough from the mold at an angle with a downward motion toward the outside of the mold. Press your index finger along the inside corner of the mold to make sure the dough goes up the side in a 90-degree angle with the bottom. Trim the top edge again, as needed. The top and the sides should be uniform in thickness.

Scraps from most rolled doughs can be recombined and rolled a second or third time. After that, they become heavy and not as flaky when baked and it is recommended to discard them. Chill and rest the dough after lining tart shells or rings.

PARLOR TRICK! Before baking, place a piece of plastic wrap loosely over the top of the tart with extra overhang on all sides. (You may need to use several sheets in opposite directions.) Top the plastic wrap with flour to snugly fill the cavity of the tart. Then, bring the plastic wrap edges to the center and twist together. Bake the tarts with the plastic wrap and flour. These will act as weights on the bottom and sides of the tarts to hold their shape. And no, the plastic won't melt. These flour pouches can be reused many times. NOTE: Make sure you use a high-grade plastic wrap that says "FOODSERVICE FILM" such as ones from Reynold's or Anchor. The grocery store brands will not work. Alternatively, you can press a piece of aluminum foil tightly around the insides and bottom of the tart to hold its shape while baking.

When your tart shells are cool, use a fine plane zester to delicately level the top rim and sides so they are perfectly flat and even.

FOLDING

Everyone knows how to stir—be it in a soup, pâte à choux or a cocktail. You go round and round and round. Just like a record. Folding is not stirring. We don't go round and round. We go under and over. Then turn. Under and over. Then turn. It's like a fancy dance move from the '80s! Folding incorporates ingredients as gently as possible. It is often used in batters and meringues where we have created volume in one portion of the mixture and want to incorporate that into another part, keeping everything light and fluffy.

Basic Procedure: Pour all the components into a very large, shallow bowl. Use a plastic bowl scraper that can easily scrape the bowl bottom and lift large amounts of the mixture at a time. From the farthest side of the bowl, pull the bowl scraper down under and through the mass, scraping the bottom of the bowl and coming up on the other side. While doing this, you are pulling batter from the bottom and folding it over the top of the mixture. Turn the bowl 45 degrees and repeat until your mixture is homogenous.

Sometimes when combining a meringue into a very stiff batter, it is recommended to "sacrifice" some of your meringue. To do this, take about a fifth of the meringue and stir it into the batter to lighten it. Although you have lost the volume of that small portion of meringue by stirring and not folding, the remaining meringue will now be easy to fold in.

When folding, pull the scraper down, under and through.

UNMOLDING CAKES

When unmolding cakes baked on sheet pans, granulated sugar is sprinkled on the top to prevent it from sticking when inverted. Since these cakes are very thin, they can often tear when removing the silicone baking mat. One way to prevent this is to freeze the cake. Another way is to use the edge of a wire rack to apply pressure on the silicone mat, folding the mat over the rack and pulling it toward you.

Basic Procedure: From about 30 centimeters (12 in) above, lightly dust the cake top with granulated sugar. Cut around the edges to break the cake away from the sides of the pan. Place a piece of parchment over the cake and flip it upside down. Remove the silicone mat slowly, starting at one corner and pulling the mat not up, but almost parallel to the mat itself in the opposite direction.

GLAZING

Desserts that will be covered in glaçage, a glaze containing gelatin or pectin, should be frozen first so the glaze will set up upon contact with the cake. Bring the glaze to the recommended temperature. Then, pull your dessert from the freezer, remove any acetate from the sides and place it on a wire rack. Pour the glaze generously over the top and sides of the cake quickly. Use an offset spatula to push the extra glaze from the top off the side. Pick up the frozen cake with the offset spatula and rub the bottom in a circular motion on the wire grid to remove any excess glaze before placing it on a platter or cake board. Any glaze that runs off the dessert can be scraped up and reheated to use again.

TEMPERING CHOCOLATE

You don't need a tempering machine. You don't need a bain-marie. You don't even need a thermometer. When we discuss tempering chocolate, we are talking about the crystallization of cocoa butter. All chocolate contains cocoa butter and therefore needs to be "tempered" to set up in a stable state. Cocoa butter can set up or crystalize in many states, but only when it solidifies in a state containing beta V crystals does it retain its shine, retract from molds and gives a snap when bitten. When chocolate is melted, this crystal structured is destroyed. If the chocolate is then simply allowed to cool and solidify on its own, it will be grainy, gray and will not have the properties of contraction that allow it to be unmolded.

The easiest way to temper chocolate is to simply not melt it all the way. Chocolate bars and pieces are perfectly tempered before they leave the factory. That means they contain stable cocoa butter crystals. When you melt a portion of the chocolate and stir it with unmelted chocolate, the stable crystals will spread and grow in the melted portion.

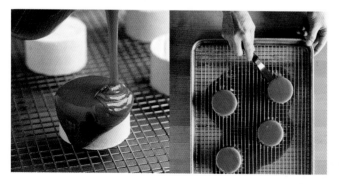

Basic Procedure: Place chocolate pieces or chopped chocolate bars in a microwave-safe bowl and place in the microwave on a low heat setting. As soon as you see the chocolate getting soft in certain areas, remove the bowl and stir. Continue to warm until about half of the chocolate is melted. Remove the bowl from the heat and continue to stir the chocolate, letting the residual heat melt the remaining solid pieces. Place back in the microwave briefly if solid pieces still remain after a couple minutes. Stir again and test for proper crystallization—place a small amount of the chocolate on the tip of a knife and wait three minutes. If the chocolate sets up without any streaking, success! If the chocolate does not set up or sets up with streaking, add a small amount of finely chopped chocolate and stir to melt without heating in the microwave. Retest and continue to add more chocolate and stir until you have a nice hard, glossy test sample.

Note the temperature of your environment. If it is above 75°F (24°C), you will have difficulties getting your chocolate to set up correctly. After using the tempered chocolate, pour any remaining onto a piece of parchment. Once cooled, reserve it for baking or ganache.

CHOCOLATE CURLS

Chocolate curls are great for adding a bit of elegance to your desserts. You can add them one by one or keep them grouped together for different effects. You will need strips of acetate that you can cut out of larger sheets or purchase already cut. Chocolate transfer sheets cut into strips can also be used.

Basic Procedure: Temper a small amount of chocolate in the microwave. Place a piece of parchment on a perfectly clean, flat counter. Space out three strips of acetate on the parchment. Cover the acetate with a thin layer of chocolate, using a small offset spatula. Run a pastry comb toward you through the chocolate. If the chocolate is still quite warm and flows back together, run the comb through a second time. As soon as the chocolate loses its sheen and starts to set up, peel the acetate off the parchment and curl it in your hands into a perfect cylinder with no overlap. If your hands are warm, try not to handle the middle. As the chocolate sets up, it will hold its shape. Allow the chocolate to sit for at least 10 minutes. If you remove the acetate too early, it will not have the shine that it should. Once set, carefully peel off the acetate. Break off the ends if they are connecting the curls. Carefully unwind the curls one by one.

> PARLOR TRICK! For perfectly round curls, you can slide your acetate into a paper towel or PVC tube while still flexible, to set up.

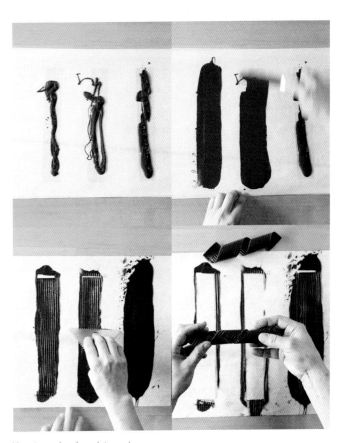

How to make chocolate curls.

SPRAYING CHOCOLATE

Chocolate can be sprayed on a frozen dessert to create a unique, velvety looking outer shell. The chocolate must be mixed with added cocoa butter to make it exceptionally fluid and reduce the chances of it clogging in the sprayer. The dessert must be frozen so the chocolate spray sets up on contact.

You can purchase a special sprayer made for chocolate or you can buy any small, handheld electric paint sprayer and dedicate it for food use.

Spraying chocolate is relatively easy as long as the chocolate stays warm and you work quickly. If you load the sprayer and let it sit for a couple of minutes, the chocolate in the gun could solidify and no longer spray. If that happens, you will have to empty the chocolate out of the sprayer and run very hot water through the sprayer before starting again. You may need to increase the pressure to help remove the clog.

Basic Procedure: Set up an empty cardboard box on the counter, open side facing you, to contain the spray. Run very hot tap water through your sprayer to make sure it is working. Dry the container and place it in an oven that was turned on briefly and then off so it is just barely warm. Prepare the chocolate spray by melting equal parts chocolate and cocoa butter. Strain the chocolate into the sprayer's container, using a small fine-mesh strainer to avoid any unmelted chocolate that could clog the sprayer. Set the pressure to about 25 psi and test it by spraying into the sink or garbage. If you can regulate the flow, open it up as much as possible.

Place the frozen dessert on a wire rack and place in the box. Immediately spray the dessert with a thin layer of chocolate from a distance of 30 centimeters (12 in), turning the rack as you go. Cover with another thin layer and repeat until you can no longer see the sides. Avoid getting too close or spraying too much at a time in one spot, or else the chocolate will not have time to set up and you may get shiny drips instead of velvet.

PARLOR TRICK! To make spraying easier and more uniform, spray the dessert on a lazy Susan or rotating cake stand.

SOAKING SYRUP

French cakes are often soaked in a sugar syrup to add flavor and keep the cake moist. This larger base recipe can be stored in the refrigerator and smaller portions can be taken and flavored differently as needed. The French call this a sirop à 30° baume, which refers to its density based on the Baume scale.

675 grams sugar
500 grams water

Place the sugar and water in a saucepan and stir to combine. Bring to a full boil. Remove from the heat and allow to cool. Store in the refrigerator.

ÉCLAIR TEMPLATE (PAGE 171)

EQUIPMENT AND INGREDIENT SOURCES

For more detailed information about equipment and ingredients used in this book, visit modernfrenchpastry.com.

INGREDIENT SOURCES AND MANUFACTURERS

ALLDRIN BROTHERS
alldrinalmonds.com
High-quality, finely ground blanched almond meal, perfect for macarons.

AMORETTI
amoretti.com
Colors, extracts, nut meals (pecan, almond, pistachio, hazelnut), nut pastes and pralines.

AUI FINE FOODS
auifinefoods.com
Fruit purees, gelatin sheets, glucose, donut/no-melt sugar, as well as silicone molds.

BORION
my-vb.com
Fruit purees and recipes.

BARRY CALLEBAUT
callebaut.com
High-quality chocolate, cocoa and chocolate pearls.

CHEFS WAREHOUSE
chefswarehouse.com
Frozen purees and quality chocolate in bulk.

CONFECTIONARY ARTS INTERNATIONAL
confectioneryarts.com
Silica gel and donut/no-melt sugar.

GOURMET SWEET BOTANICALS
gourmetsweetbotanicals.com
Edible flowers.

NIELSEN-MASSEY
nielsenmassey.com
Vanilla beans and extracts.

PENZEYS
penzeys.com
Fresh, high-quality spices and vanilla beans.

PERFECT PUREE OF NAPA VALLEY
perfectpuree.com
Fruit purees with the ability to buy direct.

VALRHONA
valrhona-chocolate.com
High-quality chocolate, cocoa and chocolate pearls.

EQUIPMENT SOURCES AND MANUFACTURERS

CHEF RUBBER
chefrubber.com
Mold making supplies, acetate, transfer sheets, colored cocoa butter and cake sparkles and glitter.

CHOCOLAT CHOCOLAT
chocolat-chocolat.com
Chocolate molds and unique chocolate boxes.

DESIGN & REALISATION
dr.ca
Chocolate molds and equipment.

JB PRINCE
jbprince.com
Molds, cake and tart rings, acetate, pastry stencils and small utensils.

KEREKES

bakedeco.com
A wide range of pastry tools, including Silikomart and other silicone molds, acetate and chocolate sprayers.

LA BOUTIQUE DES CHEFS

laboutiquedeschefs.com
A wide range of pastry tools (in French).

PASTRY CHEF CENTRAL

pastrychef.com
Tart and cake rings, Silikomart and other silicone molds, bûche de noël molds, pastry stencils and ingredients.

PASTRY CHEF'S BOUTIQUE

pastrychefsboutique.com
Edible flowers, gold and silver leaf, chocolate sprayers and Valrhona products.

PFEIL & HOLING

cakedeco.com
Dyes, colored dusts and cake boards.

RESTAURANT SUPPLY.COM

restaurantsupply.com
Matfer tart rings up to 32 centimeters (12.5 in) in diameter.

SASA DEMARLE

sasademarle.com
Silicone baking mats and molds.

SILIKOMART

professional.silikomart.com
Unique 3-D silicone molds and specialty piping tips.

THERMOWORKS

thermoworks.com
Cable extension probe thermometers and digital timers.

TOMRIC SYSTEMS

tomric.com
Custom chocolate molds.

USEFUL TOOLS AT THE HARDWARE STORE

Bench scraper

Brushes

Comb

Paint sprayer

Propane torch

PVC pipe

Ruler

Sand paper

Wooden dowel

ACKNOWLEDGMENTS

It's been a journey. Special thanks to this cast of characters . . .

ALAN—You captured the liveliness of my desserts and turned them into still lifes that look like they are still dancing on the page. Glad the kitchen did not burn up when the counter started on fire with the 151 rum while shooting the Spanish Coffee. Could have made for an interesting photo. Expensive, but interesting. Not sure whether insurance would have covered it.

TOBIAS—Thanks for successfully making my test recipes, even when you didn't always follow the directions. They all turned out delicious (whew!) and you boosted my confidence when I was running out of steam. If Tobias can make macarons, everyone can! For that, I'll share the kitchen with you again. But I still get most of the freezer space.

TEAM PIX—You held down the fort (and didn't even catch it on fire!) in my book-writing absence. Thanks for slinging the champagne and pushing out those Pixies so we could keep the customers happy and pay the bills. Although, I know the kitchen was secretly glad you didn't have to listen to OPB for four months. We missed two pledge drives. Sorry . . . I'm back! It's 8:01. The news is next.

PAGE STREET PUBLISHING—So, you sent me a random email saying, "I am really impressed with your desserts and your approach—and I also think we'd make a great book out of it." Blah, blah, blah. I had heard that before. But you were serious, and you sent me a contract. (And a check!) And together we created a piece of art. As a heartfelt thank-you, I added some extra cheese to the book. I'm from Wisconsin and we like cheese. It was an absolute pleasure working with you.

SIS—Pix dishwasher turned lawyer extraordinaire for Wisconsin's Department of Children and Families. Your skills are better used in the justice system, but thanks for the pot scrubbing and always reminding me we are Wakerhausers, thus we can do anything.

JÉRÔME DUDICOURT—Under your guidance I discovered French pâtisserie is more than science; it is equally an art. I was planning on testing recipes for Pillsbury but instead I ended up in France. Thanks for saving me from the Doughboy! He's cute and all, but you can only gussy up those crescent rolls to a point.

PHILIPPE URRACA, MOF—The opportunity to do a stage at your pâtisserie in Gimont set the path of my career. I learned not only about chocolate and pastry but also about French culture, its people and the region of Gers. Thank you for letting some random American girl encroach upon your lab and yet feel welcomed and part of the team.

MY BUSINESS PARTNERS—Visa, MasterCard and Discover. I could not have done it without you.

ABOUT THE AUTHOR

Pix Pâtisserie chef and owner Cheryl Wakerhauser (a.k.a. Pix) is known for combining bold flavors and textures into stunning, edible packages. After a short-lived career studying to be an astronaut, Cheryl headed to southern France and trained at the prestigious pâtisserie of MOF Philippe Urraca, president of the Meilleurs Ouvriers de France Pâtissiers since 2003.

Her sixteen-year-old Portland institution has been mentioned in *Food & Wine*, *Elle Décor*, *Food Network Magazine*, *Sunset*, *Wine & Spirits* and the *New York Times*, which stated, "Cheryl Wakerhauser's macarons trounce Per Se's." She is a natural teacher, explaining technique in detail but always adding a bit of pizazz and fun to each lesson, or as she calls them, Magic Shows.

Her other love? Champagne. Some women buy shoes, Cheryl buys champagne. The Pix collection has grown to over 400 cuvées that are carefully paired with Pix desserts as well as savory tapas. Cheryl's beverage list has been awarded World's Best Champagne and Sparkling Wine List three years in a row by *London's World of Fine Wine Magazine* and has won the Best of Award of Excellence for the last five years from *Wine Spectator*.

INDEX

microwaving pastry cream, 7, 32
piping ganache on cookies, 187
record player decorating trick, 96
spraying chocolate, 198
working with gold leaf, 17
pastry cream
    anise
        Soleil, 46–49
    basil
        Strawberry Fields, 54–57
    bourbon
        Miniature Bourbon Éclairs,
            170–73
    crème de cassis
        Moment of Zen, A, 38–41
    Going Bananas, 50–53
    microwaving, 7, 32, 194
    Pétanque, 156–61
    Pistachio Picnic Cake, 10–13
    vanilla bean
        Bûche de Noël, 30–35
pastry making
    success secrets for, 6–7
pâte à choux
    Confetti, 110–13
    Miniature Bourbon Éclairs, 170–73
    Pétanque, 156–61
pâte sucrée. *See* sweet tart dough
pâtisseries, 6
peaches
    Ricky Ricardo, The, 102–5
peanuts
    Concerto, 58–61
pear brandy
    Oregon Get Down, The, 36, 42–45
pears
    choosing and ripening, 43
    Oregon Get Down, The, 36, 42–45
pecans
    Bye, Bye Pumpkin Pie, 118–23
    Ricky Ricardo, The, 102–5
Pedro Ximénez sherry
    Get the Door. Pedro's Here., 85–87
pepitas
    Bye, Bye Pumpkin Pie, 118–23
Pétanque, 156–61
petits fours, 163

Baker's Dozen, 182–84
Blue Cheese Truffles, 162, 174–76
Chocolate Nougatine, 188–89
Crème Brûlée Cookies, 177–79
Earl Grey Napoleons, 185–87
Lemon Poppy Seed Macarons,
    164–69
Miniature Bourbon Éclairs, 170–73
Raspberry Almond Tea Cakes,
    180–81
phyllo dough
    Concerto, 58–61
pineapple
    ripening, 47
    Soleil, 46–49
pine nuts
    Jerez, 138–43
piping bag, using, 190
pistachio paste
    Daddy Mac, 128–31
    Pistachio Picnic Cake, 10–13
pistachios
    Daddy Mac, 128–31
    Not Your Grandmother's Bûche de
        Noël, 144–49
    Pistachio Picnic Cake, 10–13
    Sunset on the Boulevard, 62–65
plastic wrap, for baking tarts, 195
poppy seeds
    Lemon Poppy Seed Macarons,
        164–69
powdered gelatin, measuring, 7
praliné and praline cream
    Pétanque, 156–61
prunes
    Jerez, 138–43
pumpkin
    Bye, Bye Pumpkin Pie, 118–23

Q
quatre épices
    Chai, 92–96

R
Rabelo, 100, 106–9
raspberries

Confetti, 110–13
Moment of Zen, A, 38–41
Pistachio Picnic Cake, 10–13
Raspberry Almond Tea Cakes,
    180–81
When Life Gives You Lemons . . .,
    124–27
Ricky Ricardo, The, 102–5
ricotta cheese
    Not Your Grandmother's Bûche de
        Noël, 144–49
rosemary
    Bûche de Noël, 30–35
    Oregon Get Down, The, 36, 42–45
Royale, The, 132–37
rum
    Going Bananas, 50–53
    Spanish Coffee, 78–81

S
sabayon
    Baller's Delight, 88–91
Sanlúcar de Barrameda, 139
sheet gelatin, 7
sherry triangle, 139
sherry wine
    Get the Door. Pedro's Here., 85–87
    Jerez, 138–43
    styles of, 139
silver leaf
    Cancale, 20–25
    Chocolate Pandemonium, 114–17
silver luster dust
    Pétanque, 156–61
silver sparkles
    Baller's Delight, 88–91
sirop à 30° Baume. *See* Soaking Syrup
Soaking Syrup
    Bastille, 8, 26–29
    Bûche de Noël, 30–35
    Cancale, 24
    making, 198
    Moment of Zen, A, 38–41
    Moulin Rouge, 150–55
    Pétanque, 156–61
    Pistachio Picnic Cake, 10–13
    Soleil, 46–49